THE HOLOCAUST CASE

DEFEAT OF DENIAL

A Memoir with Documents

William John Cox

eLectio Publishing

Little Elm, TX

www.eLectioPublishing.com

The Holocaust Case: Defeat of Denial
By William John Cox

Copyright 2015 by William John Cox
Cover Design by eLectio Publishing, LLC

ISBN-13: 978-1-63213-160-7
Published by eLectio Publishing, LLC
Little Elm, Texas
http://www.eLectioPublishing.com

Printed in the United States of America

5 4 3 2 1   eLP   20 19 18 17 16 15

The eLectio Publishing editorial team consists of Christine LePorte, Lori Draft, Court Dudek, Jim Eccles, and Sheldon James.

Publisher's Note
The publisher does not have any control over and does not assume any responsibility for author or third-party websites or their content.

William Cox's backstory in *The Holocaust Case* strips, to the essence, the deceitful denigration of the deniers. In truth, the victorious outcome of Mel Mermelstein's breach of contract court case was never, in advance, a sure thing. Readers will learn, for the first time, about the courtroom odyssey of the courageous Holocaust survivor and his intrepid attorney as they fought their way through the precedent-setting legal trial.

Bill Younglove, Editor, *The Call of Memory: Learning About the Holocaust Through Narrative: An Anthology*

The Holocaust Case by William Cox demonstrates how determined people can fight ignorance and antisemitism. Auschwitz survivor Mel Mermelstein and lawyer Cox collaborated to bring Holocaust deniers to court and force them to pay damages. The best way to defeat Holocaust denial is to bring its lies into the open and make the liars pay.

Steve Hochstadt, Professor of History, Illinois College, and author of "Sources of the Holocaust"

CONTENTS

To the Children of the Holocaust and
To Mel Mermelstein and his family

Auschwitz (G.), Oswiecim (P.). The largest, most notorious, and murderous concentration, death, and labor camp complex located outside the city of Oswiecim in southwest Poland. It contained three major camps and thirty-six subcamps. The original and main camp, Auschwitz I, prior to its use as a concentration camp, served as a military barracks and warehouse for tobacco. It served as a concentration camp for Polish political prisoners from 1939-1942. The first inmates, 700 Polish Catholics, arrived in June 1940. Birkenau (P., Brzezinka,) or Auschwitz II (located two miles from Auschwitz I), was opened in October 1941, particularly for Jews and Roma, and was the site of four gas chambers. One hundred thousand Hungarian Jews were murdered at Birkenau in May 1944. *Dictionary of the Holocaust*

Prologue

As we walk the paths of our lives, we see and learn much along the way, and we are often faced with choices which can have profound consequences — both for ourselves and for others. At some intersections, our alternatives are limited and choices are forced upon us by circumstance. Sometimes it is difficult to remember what happened in our travels, and other times, we wish we could forget. There is, however, only one true map of our journey.

I started out as an unhappy runaway orphan boy hitchhiking down Texas highways. I had been a ward of the court since my father died when I was ten, and I was brought before the judge at age sixteen after "borrowing" my brother-in-law's 1955 Buick Century Riviera and heading for the Hill Country around Austin. When the judge asked what I wanted to do with my life, I answered that I'd like to attend the New Mexico Military Institute, if it was okay with him.

The judge approved my request, but looking over the top of his glasses, he said, "Listen boy, if I *ever* see you in here again, you're gonna be picking cotton down in Gatesville. You hear me, boy? Picking. Cotton. Down. In. Gatesville." Thus, to avoid reform school, the direction of my life shifted toward the path of discipline and a career in the justice system.

The only trouble I got into in military school was for throwing an M80 firecracker during Sunday night study hall. After I marched ninety hour-long punishment tours and graduated, I joined the Navy to "see the world."

Sent to San Diego for boot camp and Hospital Corps school, I spent the rest of my enlistment at the San Diego Naval Hospital. Ignoring my requests for sea duty, the Navy advanced me through several petty officer rates. I was assigned to supervise the tuberculosis ward, the medical records library, and finally the admissions unit of the 2,000-bed hospital.

1

Following my discharge in 1962, I worked for six months investigating insurance applicants before becoming a police officer in El Cajon, California. Upon graduation as the honor man of the San Diego Police Academy, I enrolled at the local community college and became involved in the "new breed" movement to professionalize the police service.

Two years later, I was elected president of the El Cajon Police Officers' Association. The next year, I became president of the San Diego County chapter of the statewide Peace Officers Research Association of California, representing all law enforcement officers in the county.

Perhaps as a result of my agitating for higher wages and benefits for officers, I was passed over twice for promotion to sergeant. Greatly disappointed, I was forced to choose another route in my career. A rockslide can slow you down, but it can also reveal a more interesting path.

Moving up the coast to the Los Angeles Police Department, I graduated with top honors from the LAPD Academy in 1968. My probationary period was spent on the streets of South Central LA, and then I was transferred to police headquarters for the balance of my career.

During the next four years, my personal growth accelerated. I attended law school and worked on assignments involving the analysis and application of public policy. I was privileged to write the LAPD Policy Manual and serve on the Police Task Force of President Nixon's National Advisory Commission on Criminal Justice Standards and Goals. There, I wrote the introductory chapters which defined the role of police in America, policy formulation, and community crime prevention. One of the police task force members was Joseph White, the head of Criminal Justice Planning in the state of Ohio. As an attorney and social worker, Joe mentored me in my efforts and became my friend.

The work of the commission was overseen by the Law Enforcement Assistance Administration (LEAA) of the US Justice Department, and I became acquainted with several of its administrators. These contacts resulted in my being hired as an LEAA police specialist and moving to Washington, DC.

Shortly thereafter, I was appointed the personal assistant to the director of the new Office of National Priority Programs. I quickly gained more power than I had ever imagined, as I also served as the temporary deputy and managed the office on a day-to-day basis while my boss traveled around the country.

LEAA was a funding operation with $1 billion (in 1973 dollars) to distribute each year, and I often found myself in meetings with politicians and community leaders during which promises were made which seemed impossible to keep. When I later asked how the commitments were to be honored, I was told not to be naive—there was no intention to fund.

It took only one cold winter in Washington witnessing firsthand the ruthless application of power politics to diminish the allure of a Justice Department career. Returning to my large office one day and finding my credenza covered with telephone messages lined up by time zones, I called one of my former law school professors instead.

Richard Hecht had taught me criminal law and procedure at Southwestern University, and I asked him for a job in the Los Angeles District Attorney's Office, where he served as a top administrator. He told me to come back home, so I made arrangements to leave Washington.

Although I had passed the bar examination the year before, I was not present in California for the swearing-in ceremony; however, the attorney's oath could be administered by the judge of any court of record. One of the more pleasant experiences of working on the commission was meeting US Supreme Court Justice Tom Clark and sitting next to him at a luncheon. Fortunately, we had something to talk about. He had written the majority decision in *Mapp vs. Ohio*, which established the judicial rule excluding unlawfully seized evidence, and I had written a law review article proposing a civil remedy alternative to exclusion.

Justice Clark remembered me and kindly administered the attorney oath in his chambers. He graciously signed a photograph of the event, writing, "To William J. Cox, whose voice, I predict, will be a strong one for equal justice."

Working as a deputy district attorney during the next three and a half years, I tried a criminal jury trial almost every week and was assigned to several different jurisdictions before ending up in the Long Beach Superior Court. In addition to prosecuting criminal cases, I was teaching criminal law and procedure classes at a local community college.

The practice of constantly trying cases before juries and a having a good grasp of the law gave me the confidence to take close cases to trial. The difference in a verdict often depended not only on the evidence itself, but how it was presented and argued to the judge and jury. I learned to turn my cases into interesting stories, which I told as simply and honestly as possible.

Living in a loft in Manhattan Beach with a view of the ocean, riding a motorcycle, driving a sports car, listening to music, and making movies, I was enjoying all the seventies had to offer. During the summer of 1976, however, I spent a great deal of time lying on the beach, thinking about my life and what I wanted to do with it.

Although I had considered becoming a minister in my early youth and had read the Bible several times, I had, over the years, lost my childhood faith and wasn't sure what I believed in. Watching the sun set each day, I found a different kind of faith, one that accepted the historical truth of Jesus and respected his original teaching as a basis for conduct. I considered returning to school and studying to become a minister, but decided instead to use my training as a lawyer to serve the public good.

In the normal course of personnel rotation, the District Attorney's Office had transferred me to the Juvenile Court to prosecute youthful offenders. Perhaps because of my own experiences as a ward of the court, it was difficult for me to argue for the punishment of children.

Thus, in 1977, I decided to open a public interest law practice in Long Beach, California and experiment with using the law for social and political purposes.

Once again, I found myself taking a path I had never considered before. It was to be an amazing journey.

THE PRACTICE

I had little contact with Long Beach before the District Attorney's Office transferred me to its courthouse, but I came to love the city as I walked around at lunchtime and began to meet people who lived there. With a population of close to a half million, the city has a major port at the mouth of the Los Angeles River, a school district rated as one of the best in the nation, an extensive system of neighborhood and regional parks, and a cooling ocean breeze.

With its tideland oil royalties and port revenues, Long Beach also has very well-maintained streets and infrastructures. Settled by retired Iowa farmers and home to one of the largest gay communities on the West Coast, Long Beach has a unique culture of neighborliness and liberalism. I call it the only "real city" in Los Angeles County—the larger city up the road being a disorganized amalgamation of smaller communities.

The mother of my children and I had always agreed our three children could choose to live with me when they became teenagers. My oldest, Cathy, had just married, and the middle child, Lori, had lived with me for a while before returning to her mother. When my son, Steven, reached fourteen years of age and grew to six feet tall, we decided he needed more father time. I began to search for a house in Long Beach which could serve as a home office—so I wouldn't have to commute and could spend more time with Steve.

I looked at a number of well-built (and uninspiring) California bungalows, and then the realtor showed me a three-story house that had been completely remodeled. The property had been on the market for months without any offers, and the price had been reduced into my affordability range. The problem? The house was built on a ten by forty-foot lot behind a row of storefronts.

It was love at first sight!

Designed and built by an enterprising young architect in 1932 for his wife and two children, "Skinny House" has been featured in both *Ripley's Believe it or Not* and the *Guinness Book of World Records*. It was constructed by craftsmen, who contributed their labor to showcase their skills to obtain work during the Depression. The French doors and large windows at the ends of the building gave the nine-foot-wide rooms a feeling of spaciousness. Essentially a three-bedroom house, there was enough room for living and for my practice.

I immediately bought the house.

Realizing the house had been built in the alley behind the adjoining Italian restaurant, and wanting to avoid problems with my neighbor, I formed a partnership with the Iranian owner who leased the location. We purchased the restaurant building, Steve got a part-time job washing dishes, and we had a place to have dinner each evening.

Since clients, rather than an office, make a law practice, I set about to establish my availability at a time when lawyers could not advertise. In teaching my evening classes, I always passed around a sign-in sheet at the beginning of every semester and asked my students to provide their names, addresses, and phone numbers. I contacted the clerks of the courts where I had prosecuted cases and obtained a list of the names and addresses of everyone who had served on my juries. I printed up professional announcements of my new law office and mailed them to my former jurors and students, as well as other friends I had made along the way.

I met with the presiding judges of the courts where I had prosecuted and agreed to accept appointments in adult and juvenile criminal cases where the public defender had a conflict of interest, and to serve as a judge *pro tempore* as needed.

The result of these minimal efforts was an instant law practice which handled a wide variety of criminal and civil matters. I specialized in representing juveniles accused of serious crimes.

Working with young people, I employed every legal strategy I could imagine to obtain a second chance for them to avoid the physical and emotional damage of incarceration and allow them to get on with their lives. I thoroughly interviewed my clients and investigated their cases to create their own unique stories, which I told at every opportunity in an attempt to separate them from the masses of defendants who clogged the courtrooms.

Two of these stories involved high-profile media cases in which my clients were accused of murder. The first, Anthony, arose from the horrific murders of two elderly widows during home invasions. My client was a fourteen-year-old boy who had only accompanied older adults and was not accused of inflicting any injuries himself. Even so, he was prosecuted under the felony-murder rule.

The only evidence connecting Anthony was his fifteen minute, tape-recorded confession obtained after hours of interrogation throughout the night. I attempted to prove the confession could not be voluntary under the circumstances. Moreover, I sought to establish a rule of law that the entire interrogation should be recorded if any part of it was to be introduced into evidence. (In October 2013, Governor Jerry Brown signed Senate Bill 569 which requires interrogations of juveniles in all homicide cases to be videotaped to protect against coerced confessions.)

We lost on all counts and, after appeals up to the California Supreme Court, Anthony was sentenced to the California Youth Authority until his twenty-first birthday. After serving his time, he moved out of California, established a small business, and has lived a productive life. Anthony and his mother recently visited with me, and he proudly talked about his eight children and six grandchildren.

Anthony's adult codefendant, Lloyd Earl Jackson, is still on death row in San Quentin.

The other case, Johnny, had a more successful legal conclusion, but its ending was far less happy. My client was a childlike seventeen-year-old who would watch television cartoons each afternoon after school, help his mother with dinner, and then go hang out with the neighborhood gang.

Johnny was tall, with gang initials tattooed around his neck, and the District Attorney's Office wanted him tried as an adult. We succeeded in having him found amenable for juvenile court proceedings; however, he had little or no comprehension of what was going on in court. All I could do after each appearance was to reassure him that everything was going to work out.

Johnny had accompanied older members during a gang assault on a drunk. During a police interrogation, Johnny admitted to a perfunctory kick. Someone else stabbed the victim—which the coroner ruled was the sole cause of death. The prosecutor was a friend, and I repeatedly offered to plead Johnny to an assault with intent to do great bodily harm (GBI), but the DA's office insisted on a murder conviction.

The case was heard by Los Angeles County Superior Court Judge David Fitts, who, as a deputy district attorney, had prosecuted Sirhan Sirhan—the assassin of Senator Robert Kennedy. In the Sirhan trial, Fitts presented both opening and closing statements over a period of days without reference to notes. He continued to display his great brilliance during Johnny's trial, sitting on the bench in his blue blazer, chain-smoking Marlboro cigarettes, reciting testimony, verbatim, as required, without bothering the court reporter.

At the conclusion of the prosecution, and without my client testifying, Judge Fitts found Johnny not guilty of murder but guilty of assault GBI as a necessary lesser included offense. I objected, saying it is possible to murder someone without actually assaulting them. He replied, "Be that as it may, counselor, you will have to argue that in another forum."

The judge then invited the prosecutor and me into his chambers and passed around cold cans of beer from his refrigerator. With a twinkle in his eyes, he proceeded to imagine a number of different ways for someone to commit murder without assaulting the victim. I listened carefully and made good notes as Judge Fitts laid the foundation for my appeal to "another forum."

Johnny was sentenced to the California Youth Authority, and I appealed his case. He regularly wrote letters which he closed with, "In Struggle." A copy of that signature still hangs on the wall above my desk.

On the very last day a decision could be rendered, the Court of Appeal reversed Johnny's conviction ruling that assault was not a necessary lesser included offense in murder. Because of the rule against double jeopardy, Johnny could not be retried, and the Court ordered his release. On a number of grounds, the decision became one of the most cited opinions in California jurisprudence.

Judge Fitts had obviously known he was making an erroneous legal ruling but felt he was making a judicious one to keep Johnny locked up for a short period of time for the crime he had actually committed. The judge died at the age of sixty-four in 1986.

Within a year of his release, Johnny was shot through the neck in a gang incident, rendering him a quadriplegic. I couldn't bring myself to visit him, and he died a year later. We will never know if Johnny's life would have been different had he spent more time in custody. But then, he might have been stabbed to death in prison.

I began to take an interest in political and social matters, both local and national. By combining my training and experience in policy analysis with my knowledge of the law, I worked to define alternative solutions.

The concept of policy is often misunderstood and confused with rules and procedures. Policy is derived from an analysis of knowledge and experience in relation to existing and future problems and issues. Well-thought-out policy results in broad guidelines that are easy to understand and follow.

Policy is intended to advise decision-making in difficult and complex situations. For example, the policy manual I wrote for the LAPD was the first of five volumes and included definitive rules and procedures to implement the more philosophical policy guidelines.

As a New Year's resolution on January 1, 1979, I wrote a four-page letter to President Carter saying, in part, "What concerns me…is the nagging fear that we have unconsciously failed, and that the trend of freedom has reversed. In these times of increasing dependence upon government, freedom lost or misplaced may never be regained or found."

To help "wrestle our representatives back from the clutches of special interest groups," I told President Carter I wanted "to go to the polls sometime soon and vote in a national referendum, the outcome of which could effectively guide policy-making for years to come."

I took a copy of the letter to our local newspaper, the *Long Beach Press-Telegram* and handed it to David Levinson, the editor of the editorial page. I had never met him before, and the newspaper did not publish my letter, but our paths were to become intertwined.

Eleven months later, President Carter's Director of Presidential Correspondence wrote to thank me for my interest but said that "there is no provision for a procedure [national referendum] to take place on a coordinated, nationwide basis." By then, a very busy and exciting year had passed.

In the interim, several public-policy situations had piqued my interest, commencing with the shooting of Eula Love by LAPD officers on January 3, 1979. Distraught over the recent death of her husband and because her natural gas was being disconnected for the nonpayment of her bill, Love confronted both the gas department employee and responding police officers with a butcher knife in one hand and a money order for the payment in the other. When she approached the two officers, they shot her eight times, killing her instantly. There was a public outrage.

As the author of the department's shooting policy, I was invited to appear at the subsequent Police Commission hearing. Had we considered this situation when writing policy, I testified, we probably would have advised officers to keep their distance and continue negotiating, since it was unlikely a thrown knife could inflict serious injuries.

I recommended that the department create a "Peer Review Commission" consisting of citizens and police officers to investigate and make disciplinary recommendations regarding complaints of police misconduct. The policy concept was this: "The people of the City of Los Angeles and *their* police are peers for peace."

Also in January 1979, the Long Beach Unified School District announced three vacancies on the school board and scheduled an election in April. Along with twenty-four other candidates, I decided to run for the board. I had no idea how profoundly this experience would change the direction of my life.

My platform involved some substantive changes. Considering the large geographic area of the district, I proposed its subdivision into five high school districts, each with its own board of teachers and parents to make local policy. The large district could continue to handle other matters—such as personnel, supplies, and logistics—where economies of scale applied.

As a lesson in practical politics, I enlisted my son as chairman of the "Lickem-Stickum" Committee. We sent a handwritten letter to every hundredth registered voter asking him or her to consider my platform, and, if interested, to contact his or her neighbors on my behalf.

Skinny House was designated a historical landmark of Long Beach, and we held an open house. The price of admission was as many postage stamps as a visitor chose to donate, and people lined up around the block for the chance to walk through my office. The International Year of the Child was in 1979, and we celebrated the twentieth anniversary of the

Declaration of Rights of the Child with a potluck picnic at Bixby Park, which I filmed.

I was interviewed by David Levinson and his wife, Dorothy Korber, who covered the school district for the *Long Beach Press-Telegram*. The newspaper did not endorse my candidacy, but David and Dorothy became lifelong friends.

I had no expectation of winning. During one occasion for all of the candidates to speak, I related a dream in which I won the election by one vote. I said the dream became a nightmare when I realized I had voted for myself. All of the candidates were invited to Skinny House for a glass of wine, and I became friends with most of them, including two of the three winning candidates.

Thankfully, I was not elected, but I finished respectably in the middle of the pack. Following the election, we defeated candidates got together to discuss how we could play a role in helping make policy for the district. At one of these dinners, Jane Mermelstein, who had campaigned as a teacher-candidate, introduced me to her husband, Mel.

During our conversation, Mel told me he had written a book about his experiences as a survivor of the Holocaust. He invited me out to their car where he secured a copy of *By Bread Alone* from the trunk, which he gave to me. I read it the next day while waiting in one of the long gas lines of the period and wrote him a note of appreciation and admiration for his courage and dedication. Little did I know where our exchange would lead in the future.

One evening, I discussed my idea about a national policy referendum with my new friend, David Levinson. He was a great fan of the composer, Charles Ives, who had proposed such a referendum in 1920. As we tossed ideas back and forth, the case of *Gideon vs. Wainwright* came up. Clarence Gideon, an indigent Florida prisoner, had been denied counsel in a burglary case.

Gideon filed a handwritten petition against his prison warden directly with the US Supreme Court. In 1963, in an opinion by Justice Clark, the Court ruled that state courts are required to provide counsel in all serious criminal cases where defendants cannot afford to pay for their own attorneys. It occurred to me I could send such a petition to the Supreme Court about a national policy referendum, and David thought it was "a splendid idea."

On July 9, 1979, I filed a class action lawsuit as a petition under the First Amendment directly in the US Supreme Court on behalf of all citizens, alleging our government no longer represented the voters who elected it. As a remedy, I requested the Court to order the other two branches of government to conduct a national policy referendum every four years when we elect our president.

In October 1979, Joseph White arranged for me to debate the national policy referendum with the local Republican congressional candidate at Ohio State University in Columbus, Ohio. The debate was televised by the local CUBE cable system, in which home viewers had the ability to cast instant votes through their cable boxes. The great value of the system in a debate is that the speaker can question statements by the opponent and immediately ask the audience what it thinks. At the conclusion, the viewers electronically voted sixty-seven to thirty-three percent in favor of the proposal.

Although the Supreme Court declined to hear our petition, I became acquainted with several of the journalists who covered the case. We discussed another political issue headlined at the time—the holding of US diplomatic hostages in Tehran, Iran.

Relying on my background in policy analysis, I suggested President Carter was following the wrong policy. He wanted the hostages released from the embassy so that he could bring them home. Instead, I argued he should have used international and Islamic law to get the trespassers to leave our embassy so that our diplomats could stay there and restore good relations with the country and its people.

Collaborating with the journalists, I decided to travel to Tehran, ostensibly to represent my Iranian business partner in checking on the well-being of his family. The plan was for me to go to the embassy and demand entrance to publicize the alternative policy. If I were successful in joining the hostages, the journalists—who included the Washington bureau chief of the Hearst newspaper chain—would report on my visit and the reasons for it.

Unable to obtain a visa in the United States, I flew to London to arrange travel through the Iranian consulate. Finding the offices closed for the Christmas holidays and learning it might be possible to enter Iran through Jordan, I jetted on to Tel Aviv. Arriving late at night, I took a taxi to West Jerusalem and checked into a small hotel.

Sleeping on my back, I dreamed I was asking God for a "sign." I felt a large, strong hand, like that of Saint Peter, take my right foot and slowly bend it down, painfully. I thought, "No, the bed is short and the sheets are tight. I only have a cramp in my foot." I next heard a voice calling "Wilhelm," much like my son, Steve, joked at the time, but the voice was that of Adolf Hitler.

I dreamed God not only dispenses justice but may also have a strong sense of irony. In the instant before his death, Hitler, who was Catholic, did an act of contrition and prayed for forgiveness. Since his sins were so great, however, his redemption required Hitler to serve as a small-claims judge, so long as there are Jews in Jerusalem, and to patiently listen to their most petty disputes forever.

In the dream, Hitler acknowledged his most grievous sin was the murder of babies and small children. He could never achieve forgiveness as long as there was anyone on Earth who believed his actions were justified. I awoke with the deep spiritual feeling that I had to defend the children of the Holocaust.

I found I could not enter Jordan or any Arab country with an Israeli entry stamp in my passport. With my route to Iran blocked, I returned to the United States along a different path and with a new destination.

Back home, Ronald Reagan was running against President Carter in the 1980 election. Among the other unusual things I had done during that fateful year of 1979 was to announce my own candidacy for president, just before I left for Iran.

My campaign was limited to press releases, newspaper interviews, and a late-night talk show on the local rock-and-roll radio station. My platform consisted primarily of a national policy referendum; however, I also proposed a law enforcement alternative to declaring war against nations and their people. Instead, the president should obtain a congressional "arrest warrant" for individual "outlaw" dictators, who threaten the safety of the United States and their own people. Moreover, I urged all voters to take a moment to thoughtfully write in the name of the person they wanted as their leader for the next four years, whether or not the name appeared on the ballot.

Obviously, I was not elected, nor did I vote for myself. On the weekend after the election, when the world news media was gathered in Santa Barbara at the foot of the mountain on which Ronald Reagan had his ranch, I drove there and held a press conference in the cocktail lounge of the hotel where most of the journalists were staying. Over drinks, I conceded the election and did not demand a recount.

After the press conference, I dropped off a handwritten letter at the presidential transition office at the hotel, in which I asked President-elect Reagan to consider that the USSR was not nearly as powerful as it represented itself to be. I urged him to not waste our tax dollars on an unnecessary military buildup unless he kicked a few tires and ensured the Russian missiles were real and not "Potemkin sheet metal dummies."

As 1980 ended, the full meaning and significance of the Jerusalem dream was revealed.

THE CLIENT

Mel Mermelstein walked into my office shortly after the election. As a seventeen-year-old Jewish boy, he had barely survived the Holocaust and had watched his mother and two sisters herded into the gas chambers at the Auschwitz concentration camp. Mel, his father, and his brother were selected for work. His father told them, "There's only one way for us to survive. We must stay apart, each in a different location, each away from the other. At least one of us will live to tell what they've done to us, to our children, and to our people." They separated, and Mel never saw his father or brother again.

Long before the Simon Wiesenthal Center and US Holocaust Memorial Museum were established, and during a time when most survivors tried to suppress their memories and get on with their lives, Mel collected artifacts from Auschwitz and spoke at high schools and colleges about what he had seen. A forensic psychiatrist was later of the opinion that all of "these activities were constructive endeavors which substantially ameliorated his deep pain."

In August 1980, Mel became aware of the efforts of the Institute for Historical Review (IHR) to deny the Holocaust. He wrote letters to the editors of his local newspapers and the *Jerusalem Post* accusing the *Journal of Historical Review* and its writers of spreading "lies, hatred and bigotry" about the Holocaust. He invited these "prestigious gentlemen" to accompany him to Auschwitz where he "could physically point out places where I saw the actual gassings of men, women and little children in gas chambers disguised as shower rooms."

On November 20, 1980, Mel received a letter from Lewis Brandon, Director of the IHR, challenging him to accept its offer of a $50,000 reward for proof that Jews were gassed to death in the Auschwitz Concentration Camp. The letter also said, "If we do not hear from you, we will be obliged to draw our own conclusions, and publicize this fact to the mass media."

Almost simultaneously, Mel received an "Open Letter to a Racist and Exterminationist" [sic] under the masthead of *Jewish Information*, which reproduced Mel's letter to the *Jerusalem Post*. Published in Sweden, the "bulletin" said, "Evidently you must be one of those cosmic numbers of extermination survivors who by some stroke of luck and with plenty of pecuniary stealth have survived." The bulletin went on to say the only ones to escape the "gas chambers" were "Nazi collaborators" and Mel's "sufferings have been rather lucrative." In three separate passages, it referred to Mel as a "racist."

Mel's approaches to the Anti-Defamation League and the Simon Wiesenthal Center for assistance regarding these correspondences were rebuffed with the advice that he ignore the challenges; however, he felt to do so would dishonor his promise to his father to "never forget."

When Mel asked me to help him, I did not have a choice; he was a "child of the Holocaust," one of the few who had survived.

Initially, it appeared Mel's options were limited. If he ignored the challenge, the IHR would publicize and take advantage of his failure. If he accepted, he would be judged in a kangaroo court of the IHR's own devising. I didn't have an immediate answer and told Mel I would have to think about it.

At the time, I regularly engaged in lucid dreaming in which one thinks about problems before going to sleep and subconsciously seeks solutions. I did this with Mel's dilemma and awoke in the middle of the night remembering the case of *Adams vs. Lindsell*. This 1818 English case established the postal rule—that a contract becomes valid when an unconditional acceptance of an offer is placed in the mail. Such was the law of California.

I advised Mel it was legally possible to make a binding contract with the IHR by accepting its offer. Because of the nature of the organization, it would undoubtedly default on the contract. We could then file a lawsuit in the local superior court and have the matter fairly heard there instead of in the biased IHR court.

At the time, my partner, Cheryl Bender, operated the business aspects of the practice and handled general civil and family law matters. Our associate, Dan Mangan, worked with both of us, although his primary interest was criminal law.

We agreed I would represent Mel without fee on a *pro bono* basis, which means "for the public good." Dan would help me, and Cheryl would hold down the fort.

In my optimism, I thought we could wrap up the case fairly quickly with a minimum of costs. Little did I know how rough the road ahead was or how expensive the toll would be.

THE CONTRACT

My first legal task was to make the Institute's reward offer into a binding contract. I mailed a letter to Lewis Brandon on December 18, 1980, including a completed Questionnaire and Claim for $50,000 Reward, Mel's three-page declaration about his experiences and observations at Auschwitz, and a copy of his book as an additional offer of proof. Mel's notarized signature was attached to each of these, plus his approval of my letter of acceptance.

There were two elements to our legal position. The first, under the theory of unilateral contract, was that Mel fully complied "with your requirements of proof," in that, under California law, the testimony of any one witness, if believable, is sufficient to prove any disputed fact. The second, under the theory of bilateral contract, was that Mel accepted the offer as submitted and was prepared to perform the conditions as understood.

The acceptance letter stated:

> Inasmuch as your offer letter establishes that the standard of proof shall be that which prevails in United States Criminal Courts, Mr. Mermelstein assumes that the sufficiency of his evidence will be judged by an impartial fact finder, that all proceedings will be open to public and media observation, and that the matter will be resolved in a timely manner.
>
> . . .
>
> The final paragraph of your letter emphasizes that you wish to resolve this matter 'very soon.' Since Mr. Mermelstein agrees with that premise, and shows a similar desire, it seems not unreasonable to demand that review and validation be completed in an equally timely manner as he has responded to your offer.
>
> Therefore, if no response is had by January 20, 1981, civil proceedings to enforce the contract will be instituted,

naming the Institute for Historical Review and yourself personally as defendants.

Lewis Brandon responded in a letter dated January 20, 1981, saying, "I am still deliberating on your proposal with our Committee Members and will get back to you just as soon as we have arrived at some concrete decisions."

In my reply on January 26, 1981, I said:

> We continue to consider a speedy resolution of this matter quite important in that it is the honor of Mr. Mermelstein that is daily put into question by your delay.
>
> Therefore, unless you perform in accordance with the contract in which you have now entered by February 6, 1981 we shall be forced to file an action in the Superior Court to enforce his rights.

As I had predicted, the Institute breached its contract with another letter from Brandon dated January 27, 1981:

> I have now discussed your client's claim with my colleagues.
>
> We also had another claim from Mr. Simon Wiesenthal. He wishes to claim the $50,000 for proof of gassings and the $25,000 for proof that Anne Frank's Diary is authentic. He declined to claim the $25,000 for proof that Jews were turned into soap.
>
> In the circumstances, we have decided to deal with Mr. Wiesenthal's claim for the Anne Frank Diary authenticity, and then deal simultenously [*sic*] with both his and your client's claim for the $50,000 later.

In a subsequent publication, the IHR bragged that Wiesenthal was a "most eminently suitable mouse" in its "publicity gimmick." In the meantime, later was not very soon, as originally specified in the reward offer, and the delay constituted a breach of the contract Mel entered into when we mailed our letter of acceptance.

It turned out that Lewis Brandon's true name was David McCalden. He later stated, "on the instructions of Mr. Willis Carto, the IHR's 'Agent' I was obliged to set aside my personal judgment and reverse the order of claims. This lawsuit is a direct result of Mr. Carto's instruction..."

The task now became the preparation of a civil complaint for filing in the Superior Court. I had no experience in civil litigation and feared committing an error in my ignorance which could be fatal to the proceedings. Should that occur, the even greater fear of the Jewish defense organizations about Mermelstein and his night-school lawyer would be realized. It may have appeared we were out of control, but there was a method to our madness.

THE COMPLAINT

Contract law is one of the first and more difficult subjects studied in law school. I remember feeling reassured when our professor read my midterm exam answer to the class at the conclusion of our first semester. Nonetheless, I had never considered or handled contract litigation in my practice. Fortunately, Dan Mangan was an extraordinary legal researcher. He had been one of my community college students, and he clerked for me during law school.

Dan researched the law of rewards and contracts and began to organize the complaint. We decided to combine the *Jewish Information* libel with the IHR breach of contract, as we were able to establish that the bulletin was the work of Ditlieb Felderer, one of the IHR "Committee Members."

We prepared a standard-form complaint that included breach of contract, anticipatory repudiation, libel, intentional infliction of emotional distress and declaratory relief. Something was missing, however. The very act of using a blatant lie about an established historical fact to promote a political position to the detriment of an individual should be a separate and different kind of issue than other civil wrongs, known as torts. It was like slugging a vulnerable person in the face with a lie clenched in the fist. The legal issue needed to focus on the act and intent, not the damage, as in emotional distress.

The thought occurred to me that such a fact would have to be so well-known that a court would be required to take judicial notice. One of the oldest precepts of English common law, judicial notice is based on the premise "that which is known need not be proven."

Judicial notice also became an established part of American law, and Abraham Lincoln relied upon the concept in 1858 when a witness in a murder case he was defending swore the crime took place in the moonlight. Lincoln's client was acquitted when Lincoln produced a copy of the *Farmers' Almanac* and asked the judge to take judicial notice that the moon could not have produced moonlight on the night of the event.

Accordingly, we created a cause of action titled Injurious Denial of Established Fact. The tort of Injurious Denial would specifically require the established fact—the Holocaust—to be judicially noticed as an element of the offense and as a matter of law.

Because of my great fear of making a legal mistake, we took one additional precaution after the complaint was prepared. I asked three judges with whom I had worked to privately review the complaint. They were never officially associated with any aspect of the case, but they blessed most of the pleadings we filed with the court. As a result, we never made a serious error.

On February 19, 1981, I received another letter from Lewis Brandon stating the IHR would deal with the claim at some time after November 1981. The complaint was filed on the same day.

Realizing that once you have jumped on a tiger's back, you can never get off, we organized for battle. A flow chart took up one wall of my office, laying out every step of a civil case and establishing the earliest possible dates for answers, defaults, depositions, interrogatories, demands for admissions, and motions for summary judgment.

We set about to pummel the defendants with every legitimate legal device our little law firm could generate. The defense attorney, Richard Fusilier, stated during later arguments, "Well, Your Honor, the only thing I can say is Mr. Cox has been hitting me with so many papers here that it seems obscure in my mind."

THE INVESTIGATION

Our initial pre-filing investigation revealed the Legion for the Survival of Freedom was incorporated in Texas in 1952 to aid and assist "in the promotion and preservation of American Constitutional Government." The Legion had a history of right-wing politics, including having retired Army Major General Edwin A. Walker as its secretary-treasurer in 1965.

Walker, who resigned his commission in 1961 after being reprimanded by President Kennedy for trying to direct the votes of his soldiers, led riots in Mississippi against the admission of African-Americans to the state university. Lee Harvey Oswald attempted to kill Walker in 1963, just before Oswald assassinated President Kennedy.

The Legion later merged with the Liberty Lobby, a Washington, DC corporation, and power passed from Walker to Willis Allison Carto. Carto was the initial treasurer of the combined corporation, and his wife, Elisabeth, assumed the office after 1969.

The Legion applied to do business in Los Angeles County as the Institute for Historical Review (IHR) and the Noontide Press on January 17, 1980. Legion officers were Bruce Holmon and LaVonne Furr; the application was signed by Elisabeth Carto, Treasurer. The Torrance municipal business license application was also signed by Elisabeth Carto. These individuals and entities were named in the original complaint, along with Lewis Brandon and the *Jewish Information Bulletin*.

Our attempts to serve the summons and complaint using a process server were stymied by the fact that the IHR operated out of a small storefront in an industrial area of Torrance. No sign was displayed, the doors were kept locked, and knocks were not answered.

A local private investigator was also unsuccessful in serving the papers; however, he did examine discarded trash from outside the location, and we determined Lewis Brandon's true name was David McCalden. He also used the names of David and/or Julius Finklestein.

All these efforts were consuming time, so I decided to become more personally involved in the investigation. On March 17, I did a "cop knock" on the door of the IHR, and David McCalden answered and identified himself but refused to admit he was also Lewis Brandon. Nonetheless, I handed him the papers "on behalf of yourself, Lewis Brandon, and also for the Institute for Historical Review."

Because the process server and investigator had also failed to serve Elisabeth Carto, I drove to Rancho Palos Verdes where she and Willis Carto owned a penthouse condominium overlooking the Pacific Ocean. There was no answer at the front door. I returned on March 20, and again, there was no response, so I staked out her car in the underground parking garage. She showed up several hours later and got in her car. She must have thought I was going to kill her as I approached in the darkness and seemed relieved when I served her personally and as an officer of the Legion for the Survival of Freedom and the Noontide Press.

On March 31, 1981, I informed Lewis Brandon by certified mail there would be no voluntary extension of time to answer the complaint and "If your answer is not filed with the Superior Court by April 17, 1981, I intend to take action to receive a default judgment on the pleadings."

When answers were not filed, defaults were entered by the clerk of the Superior Court on April 20, 1981 (Hitler's birthday) against the Institute for Historical Review and Lewis Brandon and on April 21, 1981 against the Legion for the Survival of Freedom and the Noontide Press.

As our investigation continued, we learned the IHR was but a small part of a national conglomerate of radical right-wing organizations grouped under the umbrella of the Liberty Lobby, Inc. These nonprofit educational entities appeared to be under the command and control of Willis Carto, who was devoted to the philosophy of Francis Parker Yockey.

A worshiper of Adolf Hitler, Yockey wrote the *Imperium* as an American *Mein Kampf*. He promoted Hitler's racially pure "high culture," which has as a primary task "the subjection of the known world to its domination." Yockey dedicated the book to Adolf Hitler, "the hero of the Second World War."

In 1960, Willis Carto was the last person to see Yockey alive. Carto describes the meeting: "as I peered through the thick screens in the San Francisco Jail, and made out the indefinite shape on the other side . . . I knew that I would have to help the prisoner as best I could . . . for the space of a fractional second, [he] spoke to me with his eyes. In that instant, we understood that I would not desert him." Later that night, wearing his Nazi jackboots, Yockey died of potassium cyanide poisoning. Carto refers to Yockey's death as "his enigmatic end."

Yockey left a note which said, "You will never discover who helped me, for he is to be found in your multitudinous ranks, at least outwardly."

Carto later published the *Imperium* to which he added a lengthy introduction. He described his meeting with Yockey: "I knew that I was in the presence of a great force, and I could feel History standing aside [*sic*] me."

Rather than retreating in the face of this far more powerful enemy, we intensified our war of paper. Based on newly-acquired information, we named Willis Carto, Liberty Lobby, and Ditlieb Felderer as defendants. Pursuant to the battle plan, we prepared interrogatories and scheduled depositions with tight time limits and served them on the defendants. We anticipated they would be uncooperative.

On May 6, 1981, David McCalden failed to appear for a deposition in my office, and Elisabeth Carto did not appear the next day. Two days later, I traveled to Washington, DC and hired two retired homicide detectives, Jack Moriarty and Richie Powers, to examine public documents and to locate Willis Carto, who had run away to that city.

Carto was confronted on the sidewalk, photographed, and personally served by the investigators to appear at my office for deposition on May 21, 1981 and to produce documents. Although the deposition was to be held within Los Angeles County, where he maintained his official residence, Carto did not appear, nor was there any communication from counsel on his behalf.

Represented by attorney Richard Fusilier, Elisabeth Carto was deposed on May 28 and declined to answer basic questions put to her, such as where she was born and her maiden name. She also refused to produce any documents as ordered. Mrs. Carto repeatedly stated, "I don't know" and "I don't remember." She did admit she was a German citizen, having arrived in the US in 1957 at age nineteen and married Willis Carto the next year.

Mrs. Carto said she did not participate in policy discussions as secretary-treasurer of the Legion. She signed checks in advance and had "no idea about money." Although, on paper, she was the superior of Brandon-McCalden, she claimed he was unsupervised during 1979 and 1980. Mrs. Carto resigned in March 1981 after the lawsuit was filed, and she no longer held office. Her only present employment was to translate German articles for the Liberty Lobby.

As a young Army soldier, defense attorney Richard Fusilier had helped liberate the Dachau concentration camp at the end of World War II. Privately, Fusilier confided he tended to believe Mel Mermelstein and did not hold a very high opinion of his clients. He had served as a Los Angeles police officer before becoming an attorney, and we established a friendly relationship.

The defaults were heard in the Superior Court on June 3, 1981. Upon Fusilier's promise to file answers and to produce David McCalden for deposition, the default and motion for sanctions were taken off the calendar.

David McCalden appeared for deposition on June 21 and proved to be a fairly cooperative witness. Whatever loyalty he may have earlier had to Willis Carto and the IHR disappeared when he was fired for making the "unauthorized" reward offer. He believed the real reason was his failure to stand up with Willis Carto during a confrontation with the Jewish Defense League outside the IHR offices.

As a witness, McCalden testified: Willis Carto also used the name Lewis Brandon; Carto was the founder of the IHR; he had hired McCalden to operate the Institute; Carto approved all decisions, including the reward offer and the rejection of Mermelstein's claim; the Mermelstein acceptance was the first proper claim; and there was no evidence to "contradict Mermelstein's allegations." McCalden had earlier written the "reward was a gimmick to attract publicity," and during the deposition, he admitted the IHR never planned to pay the reward, saying it "was never really a question."

McCalden refused to answer any questions about his background prior to his employment at the IHR. It was independently determined, however, that he had previously been the editor of the *Nationalist News* published by the National Front in England. He later became a member of the National Party and wrote for its journal, *Britain First*. The National Front was a "whites-only" political party, and its splinter group, the National Party, encouraged the return of all immigrants and their descendants to their "home" countries.

Following his split with Carto, McCalden established the Truth Missions as a competitor of the IHR and published his own newsletters. He used his involvement in the case to solicit financial support. We remained in telephone contact after his deposition, and I jokingly threatened to dismiss him as a defendant if he didn't continue to provide me with inside intelligence from the denial community.

In spite of his bigotry, McCalden had a charming wit and repartee. I kept track of him until 1990 when he died as a result of HIV/AIDS at the age of thirty-nine. He was survived by his wife and a young daughter.

Carto continued to hide out in the nation's capital, and I obtained the necessary documents from the Los Angeles County Superior Court allowing me to take his deposition in Washington, DC. He managed to elude my investigators, however, until after the time period for service expired.

To avoid drawing out the proceedings, we allowed the systematic refusal by the defendants to produce documents and answer interrogatories to pass without resort to sanctions. We wanted a resolution of the case at the earliest date.

THE BATTLE PLAN

Our strategy to obtain a prompt resolution of the primary issue—whether or not the Holocaust occurred—involved the filing of a pretrial motion for summary judgment, in which undisputed legal and factual issues are identified and ruled upon. This procedure narrows the issues and avoids the waste of judicial time at trial; however, cases are rarely decided at this stage. The best we could hope for was a fair review of the issues by an impartial judge.

The hearing on summary judgment was initially set in August 1981. As we met to discuss the case, a new volunteer joined the team. Jana Zimmer, the child of Holocaust survivors, was a seasoned attorney who brought a high level of professionalism to the effort.

It appeared we might be able to establish the contract and breach of contract, as there was no evidence in the record to dispute Mel's original declaration proving the gassing of Jews in Auschwitz. We decided, however, to put most of our eggs in the basket of judicial notice.

The theory of our created tort of Injurious Denial of Established Fact was that *the fact* was a matter *so established* that the *Court would be required to take judicial notice* of it. The legal procedure for making a motion for judicial notice involved the presentation of sufficient accurate information to help the judge *notice the fact*. In Lincoln's murder case, he handed the almanac to the judge; our task was a little more difficult.

Jana Zimmer agreed to help prepare an extensive brief on judicial notice, setting forth the law and information on which the Court could rely in making a ruling about the Holocaust. Dan worked on the law, and we began to assemble a review of the literature establishing the historical background and execution of the Holocaust. Jana concentrated on obtaining declarations from prominent historians whose field of study was the Holocaust.

I began to make midnight telephone calls to the other side of the world to Nazi hunter Simon Wiesenthal in Austria and to Gideon Hausner, the prosecutor of Adolf Eichmann, in Israel. Comprehensive declarations were obtained from both of them. In addition, I commissioned an expert literary criticism of the defendants' own publications, in case they attempted to use them as contrary information for the judge.

We prepared Supplemental Points and Authorities and Argument Regarding Corporate Liability (Appendix E) to support our position that the Legion for the Survival of Freedom and the Institute for Historical Review were responsible for the acts of David McCalden, a.k.a. Lewis Brandon.

By this time, the court file was several feet thick. In an attempt to summarize the case and clarify the issues, I created another legal device. I prepared a Notice of Request for Priority, to which I would attach my declaration providing a history and overview of the entire matter.

I sought the assistance of David Levinson. Prior to World War II, David had witnessed his father's attempt to secure safe passage of his Jewish relatives from Nazi Germany. All who failed to escape the country died in the Holocaust. As a teenager during the war, David was too young to enlist, but he now volunteered to help fight those who denied the murders of his relatives.

During one very long day, David sat at the typewriter, a cigar in the corner of his mouth, and banged out my Declaration Regarding Urgency of Proceedings (Appendix A) as I fed him information from our investigation. Essentially a magazine article, my declaration, along with the Brief on Judicial Notice (Appendix D), topped off the case before the judge.

Even though we had named Willis Carto as a defendant, we had delayed personal service of the complaint on him as a matter of strategy. He was highly offended by my declaration and could not resist filing a responsive declaration (Appendix B) in which he attacked me personally. He reaffirmed his belief in the teachings of Francis Parker Yockey as contained in the *Imperium,* implicitly threatened my life with a "loaded pistol," and asserted my membership in a conspiracy between the Anti-Defamation League, the Jewish Defense League, and the Israeli Mossad.

At about this time, I began to notice an occupied car regularly parked in the dark up the street from my office, and I received a series of late night hang-up telephone calls. One night, a voice rasped, "Can you smell the gasoline we just poured under your front door? You'd better run. We're getting ready to strike the match!" I didn't run, but I did walk downstairs and check the front door before going back to sleep.

As a former police officer and prosecutor, I took comfort in the old adage of the law enforcement profession: "If you kill a cop or DA, another one will just take his place."

As the hearing date for summary judgment approached, my real fear was making a dumb mistake. A few nights before the hearing, I had a vivid dream in which I had failed, and everywhere I went in the world, I was chased down the street by mobs of Jews yelling, "Six million victims, and you lost the case!"

THE ARGUMENT

My usual fear of failure was magnified as I walked into the courtroom on October 9, 1981. The *New York Times* had taken an interest in the case, and the lawsuit had been widely reported. Herb Brin of the *Heritage* newspaper provided the most extensive coverage of the case, and he commissioned artist David Rose to illustrate the hearing. There was an overflow crowd, and a pool camera in the back of the courtroom shared a live feed with the three major television networks.

As a trial lawyer, I knew I had to overcome my anxiety if I was to think clearly and argue effectively. I had to trust in our case preparation and believe that we would get a fair hearing and a just ruling. As always, I took a moment to close my eyes and meditate as we waited for the judge to emerge from his chambers and take the bench.

In a jury trial, an attorney ordinarily has time to prepare and rehearse opening and closing statements. During a court hearing, however, one has to answer the judge's questions and argue extemporaneously. To be effective, an attorney must not only *know* the case but *believe* in its merits.

I had never appeared before Los Angeles County Superior Court Judge Thomas Johnson. He was the presiding judge of the Law and Motion Department of the largest trial court in the United States. I had also never before tried a civil case. I was encouraged as we began to respond to the judge's questions. He appeared to be very interested in judicial notice and allowed me wide latitude in arguing the issue. (Appendix C)

I began by reviewing the ultimate conclusion of the historians' declarations "that the question today among reputable historians is not whether or not the event occurred, but rather, an analysis of why it occurred and what it means to us today."

I said, "What we have here today is a situation where if the Court is to say to the plaintiff that this is something that you have to prove as an element of your case or that this is an issue in your case, then we are in that position of the prosecutors in, perhaps, the Auschwitz trial, [or] in the trial of Eichmann in Israel . . . [T]hat would require the production

35

of a tremendous amount of evidence, perhaps so great . . . to properly prepare such an issue for determination . . . [it] would be simply beyond the ability of the plaintiff."

Briefly, I argued in favor of an established contract, but primarily directed "the Court's attention to the alleged Tort No 4 . . . 'Injurious denial of established fact.' Therein it is alleged that the . . . defendants have taken a fact of history; they have twisted it around and they have used it in order to create a great lie. They have used this great lie in a way—what they have done is they have slapped the plaintiff Mel Mermelstein in the face with this great lie. So to that extent it becomes very relevant whether or not the Holocaust occurred; whether or not it occurred in such a way as to be reasonably beyond dispute."

Mr. Fusilier responded, "I'll say that what history says and what the facts are may not be the same. Napoleon said, 'What is history but a fable agreed upon?' The crux of the situation here is they wanted someone to prove it . . . We cannot take judicial notice of a disputed fact."

Judge Johnson interrupted him, "Excuse me. We *can* take judicial notice of a disputed fact. If your lawsuit said the sun did not come up yesterday, the Court could certainly take judicial notice of that, even though that was the heart of your lawsuit." [emphasis added]

Surrendering, Fusilier said, "I agree. I am arguing—I think the Court has grasped the entire situation here. So I'll sit down on this argument, Your Honor. Thank you."

I made the basic point that, "throughout all of this literature, throughout all of the testimony, throughout the entire thirty-five-year history of our awareness of what happened during World War II, in the middle of that, nowhere in any of these trials has it been denied that . . . [the Holocaust] occurred."

Continuing, I said:

> What even the defendants say in this particular case, they say well, this was a labor thing. People were brought there and they were selected to labor in various industrial plants.

> But where did all the babies go, Your Honor? That is the question. Where did the children go? They were not subject to labor. They were not available: they were not there. And they were put to death. And that is really what this case is all about.

If that is true, then the plaintiff Mel Mermelstein at age seventeen was one of the youngest that would have survived that camp. Below him and younger than him, they did not live. They were not selected to work.

He survived that and went through an experience that neither you nor I nor anyone else who has not been there can understand and appreciate. That horrible event has to be contained within his mind. And it is embodied in this entire case, both on the one hand that it did in fact happen and on the second part that it did in fact happen and it is a part of his being. It is part of what this case is all about.

Near the end of the argument, Judge Johnson asked if I wished to "stress or highlight anything?" I had these final thoughts:

Mr. Fusilier says that since plaintiff has published one book relating to his experiences at Auschwitz, that he appears without pay and lectures at high schools and colleges, that he exercises his First Amendment rights and writes a letter to a newspaper and says who are these people; why are they doing what they are doing, that he in some way surrenders—he allows himself...to be subject to attack, some form of privilege, I suppose, some form of implied consent. This is one way of looking at this.

There is another way of looking at it. And I think it is very important to look at it in terms of the psychology, the healthiness of what Mr. Mermelstein did.

First off, we have to recognize—whether or not Your Honor grants our motion on judicial notice or not, I am not going to predicate my argument on some "as if" basis—Mr. Mermelstein went through hell. Mr. McCalden admits that. He says that Auschwitz in the summer of '44 was an incredibly horrible place. We can't detract from that. That happened.

The question is once that happened, what right have we, what privilege do we have in our own mind as to how we try to heal that? Because I think we have to just say that a seventeen-year-old boy going through that would be harmed in a grievous way.

Various people respond in different ways. But in this particular case, Mr. Mermelstein responded in a healthy way. He drafted—he wrote about it; he talked about it. But he talked about it and he wrote about it in a dignified way. He talked about it and wrote about it in a way which supported him, which supported his personal primary relationship.

He in no way allowed or by doing that said you can go into anyplace in my mind and trample around in there.

We are all entitled to open up a certain recollection or a certain memory to the extent that it can be by being exposed to the fresh air perhaps in discussion and it can somehow be made better or we can close it off. But it is our option.

That is really what this case is all about; that defendants sought out and hit the person who is in the position both in tort law and criminal law as having a paper-thin skull.

Here is someone who has tried very hard to deal with this, who has done as best he could to deal with it in a psychologically healthy way. He did in fact do that.

He has built a successful small business. He has married. He has had children. He has done well in life. And then along comes this steamroller and says no, your mother and two sisters didn't die; your father and brother, they are probably all in Russia, according to Mr. McCalden, or they are alive in Israel under assumed names.

The book of Mr. Butts that they rely on so much as being authoritative applies that Jewish people—implies that what happened is marriages were breaking down. They just abandoned their spouses and children; went off and assumed other names, garbage such as that.

But this all happened. And it did happen. And I keep having to say that. I apologize to the Court. I apologize for the record that I do not have the language to explain better, to discuss it or to describe it. But it is real.

Judge Johnson stated that he was going to take "the plaintiff's motion for summary adjudication under submission, other than the point with respect to Mr. Brandon's status as a director."

My heart sank. Was that it?

I was stunned by what he said next.

THE DECISION

Judge Johnson continued with his decision:

> But going back to the plaintiff's request for judicial notice—and I do not know that the ruling that I am going to make on that right now really determines conclusively any of the causes of action completely—I think the plaintiff's request is entitled to be complied with to this extent: Under Evidence Code Section 452(h) this Court does take judicial notice of the fact that Jews were gassed to death at Auschwitz Concentration Camp in Poland during the summer of 1944.

The judge not only took judicial notice that Jews were gassed to death in the Auschwitz concentration camp in the summer of 1944, but his ruling went further than I had ever hoped for and clearly laid to rest the most critical issue in the case. The Holocaust was simply a fact!

> Now, that is not the entire issue in this lawsuit as I see it. And in taking that judicial notice, I am not relying on offers of proof, really, by—or declaration by this plaintiff. It just simply is a fact that falls within the definition of Evidence Code Section 452(h).
>
> It is not reasonably subject to dispute. And it is capable of immediate and accurate determination by resort to sources of reasonably indisputable accuracy. It is simply a fact. It does not determine this lawsuit necessarily. (Appendix C)

As the mob of spectators and reporters gathered around my client and his family in front of the television cameras outside the courtroom, Cheryl Bender, Dan Mangan and I quietly gathered our files and left the building. It was Mel's case and his moment, and we had done our job.

The ruling was reported by all three television networks on their evening news, by most major newspapers, and it was given a two-page spread in the international edition of NEWSWEEK.

41

A few weeks later, the *Quincy, M.E.* television show presented an episode titled *Stolen Tears* in which the protagonist played by actor Jack Klugman proves the Holocaust in his investigation of the murder of an Auschwitz survivor by a Holocaust denier.

The case was not over, but any legitimate question about whether or not the Holocaust occurred was definitively answered for everyone in the world to hear—at least those who cared to listen.

THE CONFRONTATION

Recognizing that Willis Carto and his Liberty Lobby held the greatest power among the defendants and because of our limited resources, we intentionally did not serve them prior to obtaining judicial notice. Even so, Willis Carto had become a *de facto* defendant when he served interrogatories in his own name and filed a personal declaration in response to my declaration in support of our Notice of Request for Priority.

In his declaration (Appendix B), Carto complained I had "made no attempt to serve" him. Following the Court's decision on October 9, 1981, I resolved to alleviate Mr. Carto's aggravation.

Learning the Institute for Historical Review was holding its annual conference on November 22, 1981 at the Hacienda Hotel in the city of El Segundo, just south of the Los Angeles Airport, I went there with service copies of the complaint for Willis Carto and the Liberty Lobby.

In keeping with law enforcement practice and as a professional courtesy, I first stopped by the El Segundo Police Department, identified myself, and informed the watch commander of my plans. I checked into the hotel, left my briefcase in my room, and walked down to the meeting room where the IHR was holding its conference.

The doors were closed and several men were standing outside in the hallway. I told them who I was, explained my purpose, showed them the service copies of the complaint, and asked if Carto was inside. Informed he was present, I waited for him to exit rather than interrupt the meeting. Some of the men went back inside, and I struck up a friendly conversation with those who remained.

The meeting ended at noon, and I carefully watched as approximately thirty men came out of the room. None of them looked like the individual my investigators had photographed in Washington, DC at the time they served Willis Carto with a notice of deposition.

I entered the room and found Thomas Marcellus, the director of the IHR, whom I had earlier deposed. He stated Mr. Carto "had left" (apparently through a back door into the kitchen area) and would not

43

accept service. Marcellus did invite me to speak to the conference after lunch, and I accepted.

Demonstrators from the Jewish Defense League were outside the hotel building harassing delegates who were leaving. I approached their leader, Irv Rubin, to whom I had once spoken on the telephone, but whom I had never met. I told him my purpose for being at the location and said he was embarrassing my efforts. He agreed to leave, and the demonstrators departed.

After a snack in my room and a review of my notes, I entered the conference room. I did not see Willis Carto. I told the delegates my purpose for being there, but I laid the summons and complaint aside. Speaking to them personally and not as Mermelstein's lawyer, I expressed my concern that their efforts would lead to further war and violence. Although my memory is not clear on the details, I do remember telling them I practiced nonviolence and did not believe violence ever produced anything worth having.

I returned to my room, picked up my briefcase, and checked out at the front desk. As I was turning away, I was confronted by an individual who appeared identical to the photographs I had seen of Willis Carto. I asked if he was Carto, and he denied it, giving me another name.

He said, "Hey Coxey, I heard that you don't believe in violence. What would you do if someone were going to hurt you?"

I said, "Do you mean what would I do if *you* were going to hurt me?"

He said "yes," and I stepped closer, looked down at him, raised my right hand above his upturned face, the fingernail of my thumb over his right eye and the fingernail of my middle finger over his left, and whispered, "Well, I guess I would just *gouge* out his eyes."

The individual turned and walked away quickly without another word.

THE NEXT STEP

The thrill of yesterday's victory was not long lasting, as we were immediately faced with the reality of tomorrow. My small firm was emotionally and financially exhausted after working on the case virtually nonstop for a year, maxing out our credit cards and diverting our reduced cash flow into the costs of case, including transcripts, investigators, and "red-eye" flights to Washington.

Mel had done what he could to help with the costs, but he was not wealthy and, as a maverick, he was reluctant to ask others for help. An article in the *Heritage* about the expenses of the case brought in a hundred small contributions totaling $3,300. My friend, Joseph White, loaned me five hundred dollars to pay for my last trip to Washington, DC, which I later repaid.

As time passed, it became increasingly clear I would not be able to continue my representation at the level of intensity the case required. My partner, who had suffered financially, decided to go it alone, and Dan accepted a job as a deputy public defender in San Bernardino County.

I was privately retained to represent a young father accused of the murder of his infant son in a "shaken baby" case. He appeared to be completely innocent. Our agreement was that I would only represent him for the preliminary hearing and, if bound over for trial, the case would be taken over by the public defender's office.

Unusual in such matters, we presented defense testimony from a privately-retained pathologist about the cause of death and expert testimony from a child psychologist. After a weeklong hearing, my client fainted in court when he was held to answer, and I had to help carry him from the courtroom back into the lockup.

The next day, I attended yet another autopsy of the tiny baby at the Orange County coroner's office to resolve some of the issues we had raised about the cause of death. Afterward, as I drove back to Long Beach on the freeway, I sobbed for the entire distance and decided I could not go on.

I was growing more than weary of handling heart-wrenching juvenile and criminal cases under conditions where there was

45

increasingly little I could do for my clients. As I later wrote, "The justice system was in the process of being reoriented from rehabilitation to punishment. Compassion and discretion were increasingly limited by statute, and density, rather than warmth, was becoming the measure of the hearts of those who judged."

I decided to close my law office. Arrangements were made for attorney Michael Maroko, the child of Holocaust survivors, to take over the remaining aspects of Mel's case.

In my last letter to Mel as his attorney, I concluded:

> I do not know what the future holds for us. I am fearful for not only you and me but for our families. I question whether an organization that has shown continued growth over twenty years, which has grown fat by peddling hate and lies, will die out on its own. I believe that we badly wounded their effort. But we are not the scorekeepers or the spectators—we were only the players. Perhaps we were too close to the action. I don't know. I am sore and tired, but I do not feel defeated. *Shalom Aleichem.*

Without any plans for the future, I wrapped up my last few cases and retreated into solitude. I disconnected the telephones and stopped answering the front door.

My son, Steve, had returned to live with his mother. On his eighteenth birthday, I drove to Northern California and handed him the keys to my classic Volvo 1800 sports car—he had always loved the car, and I no longer needed it to get to court.

Throughout my life, I have dealt with occasional bouts of depression by productively working my way through them. Ignoring my financial situation, I spent the next year thinking and writing about philosophical and scientific matters. I imagined the concepts later set forth in *Mindkind: Math & Physics for the New Millennium* and *Time Travel to Ancient Math & Physics.*

Although the utilities were shut off and Skinny House was foreclosed upon, I never considered bankruptcy. Throwing myself into the cold, I searched for the way forward.

THE CONCLUSION

Attorney Michael Maroko did an outstanding and lawyerly job for Mel Mermelstein. With the resources of a large, successful, and respected law firm behind him, he was able to conclude the cases against all defendants.

When the matter was ultimately set for trial in August 1985, Los Angeles County Superior Court Judge Robert Wenke held a mandatory settlement conference.

In light of Judge Johnson's taking judicial notice, Judge Wenke refused to allow any evidence denying the Holocaust.

Faced with the likelihood they could be liable for millions in damages, plus extensive costs, the defendants, including Willis and Elisabeth Carto, the Legion for the Survival of Freedom, the Liberty Lobby, the Noontide Press and the Institute for Historical Review agreed to settle the case for $90,000 and to issue the following letter of apology:

Whereas, the Legion for Survival of Freedom, and the Institute for Historical Review, sent by letter dated November 20, 1985, directly to Mel Mermelstein, a survivor of Auschwitz-Birkenau and Buchenwald, an exclusive reward offer in a letter marked 'personal' dated November 20, 1980, offering Mr. Mermelstein a $50,000 exclusive reward for 'proof that Jews were gassed in gas chambers at Auschwitz' and further stating that if Mr. Mermelstein did not respond to the reward offer 'very soon' the Institute for Historical Review would "publicize that fact to the mass media..."

Whereas, Mr. Mermelstein formally applied for said $50,000 reward on December 18, 1980; and

Whereas, Mr. Mermelstein now contends that the Institute for Historical Review knew, or should have known, from Mr. Mermelstein's letter to the editor of the *Jerusalem Post* dated August 17, 1980, that Mr. Mermelstein contended he was a survivor of

Auschwitz-Birkenau and Buchenwald; that his mother and two sisters were gassed to death at Auschwitz; and knew, or should have known, of his contention that at dawn on May 2, 1944, he observed his mother and two sisters, among other women and children, being lured and driven into the gas chambers at Auschwitz-Birkenau, which he later discovered to be Gas Chamber No. 5; and

Whereas, on October 9, 1981, the parties in dispute in the litigation filed cross-motions for summary judgment resulting in the court, per the Honorable Thomas T. Johnson, taking judicial notice as follows:

"Under Evidence Code Section 452(h), this Court does take judicial notice of the fact that Jews were gassed to death at the Auschwitz Concentration Camp in Poland during the summer of 1944, and it just simply is a fact that falls within the definition of Evidence Code Section 452(h). It is not reasonably subject to dispute. And it is capable of immediate and accurate determination by resort to sources of reasonably indisputable accuracy. It is simply a fact."

Whereas, Mr. Mermelstein and other survivors of Auschwitz contend that they suffered severe emotional distress resulting from said reward offer and subsequent conduct of the Institute for Historical Review; and

Whereas, the Institute for Historical Review and Legion for the Survival of Freedom now contend that in offering such reward there was no intent to offend, embarrass or cause emotional strain to anyone, including Mr. Mermelstein, a survivor of Auschwitz-Birkenau and Buchenwald Concentration Camps in World War II, and a person who lost his father, mother, brother and two sisters, who also were inmates of Auschwitz.

Whereas, the Institute for Historical Review and Legion for the Survival of Freedom should have been aware that the reward offer would cause Mr. Mermelstein and other survivors of Auschwitz to suffer severe emotional distress which the Institute for Historical Review and Legion for the Survival of Freedom, now recognize is regrettable and abusive to survivors of Auschwitz.

Each of the answering defendants do hereby officially and formally apologize to Mr. Mel Mermelstein, a survivor of Auschwitz-Birkenau and Buchenwald, and all other survivors of Auschwitz for the pain, anguish and suffering he and all other Auschwitz survivors have sustained relating to the $50,000 reward offer for proof that "Jews were gassed in gas chambers at Auschwitz."

The following year, in January 1986, the Los Angeles County Superior Court heard the remaining issue of libel by defendant Ditlieb Felderer, who did not appear. The jury returned a verdict of $500,000 in compensatory damages and $4,750,000 in punitive damages. Felderer was later criminally convicted of denying the Holocaust in Sweden and was jailed in 1994. The judgment remains unsatisfied.

Although additional litigation regarding other issues between Mel Mermelstein and Willis Carto would take place in the future, the case we originally filed in February 1981 was successfully concluded in 1986.

Michael Maroko provided highly competent professional representation for Mel Mermelstein and other Holocaust survivors, and I am forever indebted to him for lifting the load when I could no longer bear it.

As the original case was played out, I walked on alone, unaware of the danger that lurked around the bend.

THE AMBUSH

More than a year and a half passed since my confrontation with Willis Carto at the IHR conference. Then he suddenly struck without warning, but not up close where I could defend myself.

On June 24, 1983, I received a summons and complaint by certified mail regarding a new lawsuit Carto had personally filed in the US District Court in Washington, DC. The complaint named me as the primary defendant, and included Melvin Mermelstein, Auschwitz Study Foundation, Inc.; Herbert Brin, Heritage Publishing Company; and Irv Rubin, Mordechai Levy, and the Jewish Defense League (JDL).

As the publisher of the *Heritage* newspaper, Herb Brin had provided the most in-depth coverage of the Holocaust Case, and the Auschwitz Study Foundation was Mel's nonprofit that operated his small Holocaust museum. The JDL had no involvement in the case.

The complaint identified Carto as a citizen of the District of Columbia and the treasurer of the Liberty Lobby, which was headquartered in the same city. It was signed by Fleming Lee, the general counsel of the Liberty Lobby, with whom I had originally spoken when trying to determine why Carto was not appearing for his deposition in the Holocaust Case. At that time, Lee denied he represented Carto.

The complaint alleged abuse of process, intentional infliction of emotional distress, invasion of privacy, and defamation. Exhibits attached to the complaint included the amended complaint in the Holocaust Case filed on November 4, 1981 after the Judicial Notice hearing and my Declaration Regarding Urgency of Proceedings, which was Carto's primary complaint. Paragraphs 47, 48, and 49 of his complaint stated:

> The false, malicious, and defamatory statements contained in the Cox "Declaration" were not relevant to the lawsuit in which they were filed. The "Declaration" was unrelated to the issues in that case, served no

legitimate procedure or substantive purpose, and contributed nothing to the pursuit of the remedies sought by Melvin Mermelstein. Willis Carto was not a litigant in the lawsuit in which the "Declaration" was filed.

William Cox deliberately sought and achieved excessive publication of his "Declaration" outside the lawsuit in which it was filed. The actual purposes of the "Declaration" were propaganda and publicity.

Plaintiff further alleges that upon information and belief, defendant Cox was assisted in the preparation and writing of the aforesaid "Declaration" by persons whose individual identities are at this time unknown to plaintiff, but who aided Cox as a part of a pattern of defamation of the plaintiff, and who were motivated by a malicious desire to harm the plaintiff through spreading calumnious falsehoods about him.

Although Carto's complaint alleged all defendants were agents of each other in a "mutual goal of unlawful damage to the plaintiff," the alleged acts of the "conspiracy" were primarily those I had done in handling Mel's case, plus independent actions of the JDL and the articles in the *Heritage* newspaper, which were unrelated to my prosecution of the case.

An amended complaint filed three weeks later on July 12, 1983 deleted the Jewish Defense League, Irv Ruben, and Mordechai Levy from the complaint but retained all of the alleged conspiratorial acts associated with them.

Mel Mermelstein and Herb Brin were quickly represented by *pro bono* counsel in Washington, DC. Because practically all of the actions complained about (except for those attributed to the JDL and the *Heritage*) had been taken by me in the prosecution of the case, I believed there would be a conflict of interest for me to share the same attorney. A legitimate defense for Mel and Herb would have been to shift the blame to me.

On behalf of Brin, Mermelstein, and their organizations, their Washington counsel filed a Rule 12(b) motion to dismiss the complaint based upon jurisdictional grounds. That motion was quickly granted.

At that point, it was just Carto and me left in the lawsuit. He had his in-house lawyer, and I was unrepresented and no longer practiced law. All of my attempts to obtain representation failed. I was forced to represent myself in a forum 2,700 miles from my home, which was about to be foreclosed upon. I no longer had a car or a telephone, and I had no money for secretarial services or airfare.

My hero, Abraham Lincoln (whose photograph hangs on the wall above my desk), once said, "He who represents himself has a fool for a client," and I set about to prove him right. After obtaining several continuances, Fleming Lee set a deadline of September 1, 1983.

Instead of answering the complaint, I prepared three motions under the Federal Rules of Procedure. The first was a Motion for Judicial Notice regarding documents from the Los Angeles court file. The second, under Rule 12(b) (Appendix G), was similar to that filed by the co-defendants which resulted in the case against them being dismissed. My declaration established my only contacts with Washington, DC were those related to prosecuting the case and that Carto's proper residence was in Los Angeles County, where the original case was still pending.

The third pleading, under Rule 11, was a Motion to Strike Signature of Complaint (Appendix F). It alleged:

1. The bringing of the complaint involved wrongful motivation of the plaintiff to the extent that it constitutes a fraud upon the Court and a criminal contempt of its dignity and purpose.

2. Counsel for the plaintiff does not enjoy the independence normally expected of an officer of the Court in that he is an employee of the plaintiff, he serves in a subaltern role, does the express wrongful bidding of his client, and conducted no independent investigation of the circumstances before filing the instant complaint.

Paragraph seven of my declaration in support of the Rule 11 motion stated:

> The headquarters of the Liberty Lobby at 300 Independence Avenue is an old, converted mansion connected by a rabbit warren of passages to other buildings adjacent to the east. Within these confines, Willis Carto is the virtual dictator, making all decisions

and directing all operations. Counsel for Willis Carto in this action, Fleming Lee, is the general counsel of the Liberty Lobby, and in that role, works directly for and under the supervision of Willis Carto. Given the bunker mentality that exists there, Mr. Lee would be fired if he disagreed with Mr. Carto.

I mailed the three motions to the court on August 31, 1983 and served copies by mail on Carto's attorney at their Washington, DC address. The following dates and their sequence are important.

The next thing I received regarding the case was the Plaintiff's Motion for Order Extending Time in Which to Respond to Motions of Defendant Cox with Incorporated Statement of Points and Authorities which was signed and dated September 12, 1983. In it, Mr. Lee stated in part:

> This motion for an extension of time of approximately ten (10) days should be granted because defendant Cox's motions and the voluminous assortment of documents which accompanied them did not arrive at undersigned counsel's office until September 7, 1983, even though they were mailed by September 1st... Because of the belated arrival of the papers, plaintiff would be deprived of a fair and reasonable time in which to respond unless the deadline is extended.
>
> Furthermore, the lengthy and unusual nature of defendant Cox's motions and their unorthodox adjuncts will require more than ordinary time to prepare a response.

Within a day or so, I received a notice dated September 13, 1983 from the court clerk returning my Rule 11 and Rule 12(b) motions with the instruction that I "correct the order of the motions. Copies are missing pages and incomplete. Two motions are incorporated in one pleading."

Apparently, not only acting as my own lawyer but as my own secretary as well, I had committed the very type of clerical mistake I had worked so hard to avoid in the Los Angeles case.

I corrected the errors and resubmitted the two motions on September 23, 1983. They were received and filed by the court on September 27, 1983.

I was waiting for Carto's response to my revised motions and heard nothing further until I received a Motion for Entry of Judgment by Default on November 7, 1983. The motion was filed on November 3, 1983, more than a month after my motions were successfully filed with the court; however, it stated the actual default had been entered on September 15, 1983, five days after Carto requested a ten-day continuance. I never received a notice that the default had been filed.

Carto had his revenge!

Apparently, when Carto's attorney went to file his request for an extension to answer my original motions, he discovered my original Rule 11 and 12(b) motions had been rejected by the court clerk. Whereupon, a default was quickly entered the next day. Once the default was in place, my later filing of the corrected motions would not be considered by the court, unless the default was set aside.

Ordinarily, courts routinely set aside defaults for minor errors, such as making a mistake in filing response papers; however, by the time I found out Carto was seeking a judgment, I no longer had the energy or means to do anything about it.

Carto's Motion for Entry of Judgment by Default requested a judgment of $4,200,000. I never received any documents regarding the actual judgment, but I've since learned the court ordered the nominal sum of $2,500.

I have at all times ever since maintained a current address with the State Bar of California; however, Carto has never, to my knowledge, sought to enforce his judgment. Perhaps it is because I was judgment-proof, without assets at that time, or perhaps the unsatisfied judgment carried a greater propaganda value than its collection.

Carto and I went our separate ways in 1983. Because of events that lay in the future, his path became more difficult, while mine became easier.

THE COMEUPPANCE

As we have seen, the Institute for Historical Review was founded by Willis Carto and David McCalden, its first director. As the IHR's agent, Carto had the power to hire and fire the director, which he did. Carto replaced McCalden with Tom Marcellus in an attempt to shift liability to McCalden for making the original reward offer to Mel Mermelstein.

Carto's control of the IHR was also maintained through his wife, Elisabeth Carto, who served as the treasurer and signed the initial business license and fictitious business name documents allowing the Texas-based Legion for the Survival of Freedom to do business in California as the Institute for Historical Review. His grip became less firm when she resigned at the outset of the Holocaust Case.

Carto's ability to exercise power over the Legion, as the IHR's parent corporation, was based upon his personal relationship with the Legion's board of directors, primarily LaVonne Furr and her husband, Lewis. (LaVonne was originally named as a defendant in the Holocaust Case.) The elderly couple, who had been associated with Carto since 1964, lived in Arkansas and had little or nothing to do with the day-to-day operations of the Legion or the IHR.

At some point after the Holocaust Case, Carto augmented the IHR staff with the addition of Mark Weber and several other employees. Weber was later described by Carto in a declaration dated January 6, 1994, as having "once worked for William Pierce and his openly Nazi National Alliance."

In what Carto was to call a *coup d'état*, Marcellus, Weber, and the other employees orchestrated Carto's own dismissal as the IHR's agent in October 1993.

According to the *Los Angeles Times*, the IHR employees "criticized Carto for botching the handling of the celebrated Mermelstein case" and "blamed Carto, too, for economizing on the institute's fire insurance coverage, which became a compelling issue after the group's former quarters in Torrance were destroyed in a July 1984 firebombing that caused $300,000 in damages. The premises were insured for only $50,000. One employee bitterly observed in a court declaration that only

Carto's locked personal office—which contained four heavy bronze busts of Hitler—was unscathed by fire."

The *Times* quoted Weber as saying Carto "wanted to make substantive changes in the direction of the review. He wanted it to become more 'racist,' to make it more clearly white racist." Marcellus wrote in a declaration, "Having suffered Carto's machinations, hair-brained [sic] schemes, mismanagement, insults and irrationality long enough, the senior staff met to determine the course of action to stop Carto from taking harmful actions."

Money, rather than ideology, proved to be the primary issue when the IHR employees discovered the existence of a legacy from Jean Farrel Edison, the granddaughter of Thomas Edison. She died in 1985 and left control of access to cash certificates valued at up to $40 million to the Legion. Following litigation in Switzerland, the Legion reportedly received a $10 million settlement, over which Carto took custody. According to the *Times*, Carto established Vebit, Inc., a separate corporation, "to control the money and loan it back to the Legion."

The IHR senior staff persuaded the elderly Furrs to resign from the Legion board and enlisted the remaining director to appoint a "slate of new directors in the rebel camp." The new Legion board then fired Carto.

A flurry of lawsuits and cross complaints were filed in the California courts to secure control of the Legion, the Edison legacy, and the IHR's inventory of books. Ironically, one issue in the case resulted from Carto's earlier attempt to avoid financial liability in our original Los Angeles case. At that time, he transferred the book inventory to a new unincorporated association, called the Historical Education Foundation (HEF), as collateral for a "loan" of $187,000. The rebel board repudiated the HEF note and moved the books to a new location.

Although Carto fought back in court, he also took direct physical action on October 15, 1993. What occurred that day depends upon whether one reads the IHR's account or Carto's version, but the *Los Angeles Times* described it thusly:

> While the editors were away, Carto notified their attorney that he was seizing control. Meanwhile, according to remaining staff members, Carto and his wife and three men set about disconnecting the office

telephones, disabling the computers and changing the locks.

"It was hard to keep from laughing," recalled Hulsey, the staff attorney who raced to the office after receiving the faxed declaration of war. "It was like something out of Woody Allen's Banana Republic. Who would control the headquarters? The staff arrives, forces the door and then fistfights start breaking out all over."

Eventually police arrived and Carto was arrested along with some of the other staff members. Charges were never filed against any of them.

Hulsey's last memory of the melee is an indelible image of Willis Carto with one foot wedged in the door. Nearby a staff editor brandished a gun to break up a wrestling match on the floor. Meanwhile, other institute historians were struggling mightily to shove Carto out the door.

The founder's screams filled the room: "You're killing me!"

The Institute ultimately obtained a $6,430,000 judgment against Carto in 1996 resulting from its lawsuit, which alleged he had embezzled $7.5 million of the Edison legacy.

Judge Runston Maino of the San Diego County Superior Court found that, as a witness, Carto could not be relied upon. The judge said Carto was "evasive and argumentative" and his testimony "made no sense . . . By the end of the trial, I was of the opinion that Mr. Carto lacked candor, lacked memory and lacked the ability to be forthright about what he did honestly remember."

On July 30, 2002, Judge Maino issued an assignment order which ended the existence of the Liberty Lobby. All assets were assigned to the Legion for the Survival of Freedom including "any and all proceeds due from any Trust or Probate, wherever located, which is payable to any of the Judgment Debtors, Liberty Lobby, Inc., Willis Carto and Elisabeth Carto, which are presently due or to become due in the future."

On March 26, 2003, the Swiss government completed a lengthy investigation of Carto's involvement in the Edison legacy and issued a warrant for his arrest. It ordered the Swiss judicial police to seize Carto and detain him on charges of "abuse of trust, disloyal management and money laundering."

The 88-year-old Carto may have been knocked down, but he was not out. As of 2015, he continues to operate two new enterprises in competition with his former organizations. The *Barnes Review* is an online "magazine and book shop" that offers some of the same titles as the IHR and Noontide Press, and the *American Free Press* appears to be a journalistic replacement for the Liberty Lobby *Spotlight*.

The IHR continues to do business in Orange County as "an independent educational research and publishing center," and it no longer publishes the *Journal of Historical Review*.

In 2005, Mark Weber, IHR's current director, stated "that outright lies about Hitler and Third Reich Germany are widespread and unchallenged in today's America. The portrayal of Hitler and his regime is grotesquely unbalanced, not only in the mass media, but even in supposedly authoritative history books and reference works."

I last heard from Carto in 2009 in an email regarding an article I had written about James von Brunn, who had murdered a guard at the Holocaust Memorial Museum in Washington, DC. Brunn had once worked for the Noontide Press and expressed an admiration of Carto. In his email, Carto said, "Cox, you are a liar on many counts . . . I am contacting a reputable attorney to see how much of your garbage is actionable. Why don't you get a life?"

In addition to his suit against me in 1983, Carto filed many lawsuits over the years for defamation, some of which were dismissed when he refused to participate in meaningful discovery. Other matters were dismissed upon summary judgment, when he, as a public figure, was unable to prove actual malice. A couple were settled for nominal amounts.

Carto's primary libel complaint usually has to do with his being called a Nazi or racist, and it appears he wants to have it both ways. He wants to be able to hire Mark Weber, a former member of the National Alliance on one hand, and later accuse Weber of having worked for that "openly Nazi" organization after they have a falling out.

A recent book offered by Carto's *Barnes Review* is *Hitler's Revolution*. A review on the website says the book about "the greatest man of the 20th century" is "both refreshing and full of surprises even for the seasoned student of Hitler." Years ago, Carto wrote an introduction to

Imperium, which is dedicated to Adolf Hitler, and there were those four bronze busts of Hitler in his private IHR office. Nonetheless, he is quick to sue if called a Nazi.

In the *Imperium* introduction, Carto demands "a racial view of history," and proclaims that "the genetic interpretation of race is a necessary, useful and valid one if we are to see all of our problems clearly and accurately." He says, "Negro equality or even supremacy . . . is easier to believe in if there are no Negroes around to destroy the concept." He reaffirmed his admiration of *Imperium* in his own declaration (Appendix B), yet he cries "slander" if called a racist.

I have no malice, whatsoever, toward Willis Carto, nor do I desire to go through another lawsuit with him. I am sure he believes what he says about his view of history, and I believe he has a First Amendment right to say and publish it. I do not, however, believe he can legally do so, for his own personal motives, in a manner that specifically targets and harms another individual. That is malicious. I, too, have a First Amendment right to recount the history of our encounter from my point of view, as he did in the book, *Best Witness: The Mel Mermelstein Affair and the Triumph of Historical Revisionism*. I cannot allow his threats to intimidate me.

Willis Carto and I are both in our twilight years, and the time approaches when we will each reach the end of our individual paths. I wish him no harm in the remainder of his journey. I only wish he could say the same for me, but I don't think Carto will ever want to become my fishing buddy.

THE RECOVERY

In 1984, retired LAPD Deputy Chief Vern Hoy contacted me about the possibility of coming to work with him and his partner, retired LAPD Commander Frank Brittell. Chief Hoy had supervised my writing of the Policy Manual and was the executive director of the police task force I worked on in the early seventies. After retirement, he went on to serve a five-year term as the Director of the Arizona Department of Public Safety. Commander Brittell was the original leader of the LAPD Special Weapons and Tactics (SWAT) team. Hoy was one of the most cerebral thinkers ever produced by the department, and Brittell was one of its best known tactical field commanders.

They had come together to form Brittell and Hoy, Inc. (BHI), whose clients included a host of Fortune 500 companies, as well as the nuclear weapons sites operated by the US Department of Energy. They also had a subsidiary company, Centurion Research, which did background investigations for the nuclear power industry. The BHI workload had increased to the point where they needed administrative help.

I served as the BHI general counsel and operations officer until the corporation was purchased by a group of investors. I remained with the resulting Business Risks International (BRI) corporation as it continued to buy up a number of other security consulting and investigation companies and ultimately opened offices in most major cities. These two companies established policy, philosophy, and practices which set the standard for professional protection in the burgeoning private security industry.

Making use of the highly-computerized operations I learned at BHI and BRI, I opened an "investigative law office" in 1988 in Long Beach to offer specialized legal services, primarily to other attorneys.

In 1991, actor Leonard Nimoy of *Star Trek* fame produced a movie for Turner Network Television about the Holocaust Case. Titled *Never Forget*, the film starred Nimoy as Mel Mermelstein and Dabney Coleman as me. In his autobiography, *I Am Spock*, Nimoy said, "If every project brought me the same sense of fulfillment that *Never Forget* did, I would truly be in paradise. For me, Mel's story goes beyond the Nazi/Jewish issue, beyond the horrors of Auschwitz; it addresses the fundamental issues of the human spirit."

Nimoy's performance was compelling and could actually convince me that he was Mel; however, even though Coleman movingly spoke the actual words I used in arguing the case, it was impossible for him to convince me that he was me.

I had maintained friendly contact with defense attorney Richard Fusilier over the years, and he telephoned me the morning after the movie was aired by TNT. He said, "Cox, I never knew I was such a bad guy." Fusilier resigned from the State Bar of California with disciplinary charges pending in 1995, and he died in 2012.

I used the money I received for the movie rights to pay off the remaining debts I had left over from the Holocaust Case.

In 1991, I became involved in another high-profile *pro bono* matter. Representing a secret client, I arranged publication of the long-suppressed Dead Sea Scrolls by the Biblical Archeology Society. I obtained legal possession of 1,800 photographs of the scrolls and signed a contract on behalf of my client for their publication. When called to testify in the resulting trial in Jerusalem, I refused to identify my client, whose identity remains privileged.

I lived and practiced law in an inexpensive Ocean Boulevard apartment overlooking the entrance to Long Beach Harbor. Working about one case a month to pay the rent, I continued to develop the principles of universal physics, mathematics, and geometry and to imagine the philosophy of Mindkind.

Late one evening as I was returning to my apartment by a dark side street, I was jumped by two robbers. Had they asked, I probably would have handed over my wallet; however, one hit me in the face with a bottle of wine before breaking the bottle over the top of my head. My police training kicked in, and I went into full fury, fighting them off and yelling for help. As they finally turned away, I yelled at them to run before picking up my broken glasses and continuing to my apartment.

Covered with blood, I drove to the emergency room where I was stitched up like a baseball. After looking at the X-rays of my thick skull, the doctor said, "They only thought they were going to hurt you by hitting you on the head."

Other than adding a few more scars to my already battered face, the primary consequence of the event was my adoption of a dog. "KD" was a mixed-breed German Shepherd and Dingo with big ears and a lovely gold and white coat. Having worked with a police dog on the El Cajon Police Department, I trained KD to accompany me everywhere I went. Although I did not give her attack training, she wore a professional leather harness and appeared to be a working dog. Nobody ever stopped us or interfered with our progress.

KD and I began to go to the Long Beach Dog Park every day, where she would perform her signature trick of leaping up to catch a tennis ball and spinning 360 degrees before landing. This is how I met Naomi, a second-grader, who always wanted to throw the ball up, over and over. One Saturday morning, her mother was there alone. When I asked Helen where Naomi was, she replied it was "her weekend with her father." Sensing an opportunity, I immediately asked Helen for a date, and the rest is history.

In a three-ring ceremony (one for Naomi), Helen and I were married on Valentine's Day 2000 in Christ Church in the old city of Jerusalem.

A very practical Yankee, Helen earlier told me I had to get a "real job" if we were to get married. Thus motivated, I had found employment at the State Bar of California in 1999. I worked as a prosecutor until my retirement in 2007.

Serving as a supervising trial counsel of the State Bar, I led a highly professional team of investigators and attorneys. We targeted the prosecution of attorneys accused of serious crimes and misconduct. We were so successful that the California legislature expanded our authority, allowing us to take on non-attorney criminal gangs engaged in the illegal practice of law.

Since retirement, I have written articles and books about philosophical, political, and social matters. As my literary path wound back to the beginning, it seemed the time was right to finally talk about the Holocaust Case.

EPILOGUE

Little had been written about Holocaust denial at the time of our case. Since 1981, though, the subject has received a great deal of attention. "Holocaust denial" currently Googles more than a million results. A number of books have been published on the subject; most of these are listed in this book's bibliography.

The case awakened new interest in the Holocaust and encouraged the subsequent publication of dozens of autobiographies and memoirs by survivors.

Actual factual evidence of the Holocaust, particularly the operation of Auschwitz II-Birkenau as an extermination facility, continues to accumulate as more and more records are uncovered by historians, which clearly document the camp's existence and murderous purpose.

The Genocide of European Jewry by Hitler's regime is an established historical fact, as was the systematic mass murder of the mentally ill and disabled, Gypsies, homosexuals, political dissidents, prisoners of war, Slavs and slave laborers by the Nazis. Altogether, as many as 26,000,000 victims may have perished in the slaughter.

Even so, Holocaust denial continues to be used as a political weapon. Former Iranian President Mahmoud Ahmadinejad once cited Holocaust denial as one of his greatest accomplishments.

Adolf Hitler, himself, never denied his "Final Solution."

Hitler spoke openly about "the annihilation of the Jewish race in Europe" and the "extermination of Jewry in Europe." Near the end of the war, he said, "many Jews are quite unaware of the destructive nature of their very existence. But whoever destroys life courts death, and that is exactly what is happening to them!"

Although he lost the war, Hitler almost accomplished his objective of exterminating European Jewry. I do not seriously believe Adolf Hitler was capable of remorse, much less performing a valid act of contrition as I once dreamed. Most likely, his state of conscience would have been similar to that of another Adolf. Eichmann stated during his trial in Jerusalem, "Repentance is for little children."

Eichmann, who readily admitted organizing the wholesale deportation of entire communities of Gypsies and Jews to what he knew was certain death, was totally devoid of any comprehension that what he did might have been wrong. It was not only that he was following orders. Rather, he was simply obeying the law. Eichmann and the thousands of other functionaries in the military and governmental bureaucracy were just doing a tough job. It was the law, and they were law-abiding.

President Obama is currently ordering the killing of people, including American citizens, every week, based on a mere suspicion they are engaging in terrorism. These murders are conducted remotely by drone attacks or during nighttime home invasions by special forces extermination teams. These troops are just following the orders of their commander-in-chief, Barack Obama, who bases his authority on a Justice Department legal opinion. The ruling holds that a determination by "a well-informed high-level administration official" (i.e. the president) that the target represents an imminent threat to the United States is sufficient justification to kill. An imminent threat does not require clear evidence that a specific attack on US persons will take place in the immediate future, and any innocent children killed or maimed in the attack are justifiable "collateral damage."

Today, we live in an era of intensive governmental surveillance in the war on terrorism, and we glorify our military. Our warriors do the tough jobs that have to be done, including drone operators who fire missiles into houses occupied by suspected terrorists and their wives and children. We are callous to such collateral damage to babies and the horrendous birth defects they suffer from our use of depleted uranium shells and chemical weapons, such as white phosphorus.

We are engaged in a never-ending war sponsored and encouraged by the military, industrial, intelligence, and homeland security complex. The existence of this shadowy power, and its encouragement of a super-patriotic culture to justify its vast expenditures, has brought the United States to the brink of fascism. In addition to the loss of the worthy things—such as health care and education—these funds could contribute to our society, the price we civilians are asked to pay is our freedom, our conscience, our empathy, and our humanity.

Not only must we never forget the inhumanity demonstrated during the Holocaust, but we must also recognize the parallel attitudes, beliefs, and actions existent in the present endless, worldwide war on terrorism.

We must identify and combat the dangers posed by the dehumanization of *anyone*, regardless of race, religion, culture, social condition, or military necessity.

At the time *Never Forget* was first shown in 1991, I wrote a letter to the *Heritage* newspaper, which closed:

> Finally, as I argued to the court, if the Holocaust did not occur, then where are all the children? Where are the babies?
>
> Why did I do it? I did it for the murdered children, whether they were Jewish, Gypsy, or Christian. Why? The world has never seen such evil. It can never happen again.
>
> Recently, I was out at Mel's and he had just received several boxes of artifacts from Auschwitz. As we stood together and looked at the pile of rusty and melted scissors, spoons and forks, and other items taken from the victims and later burned, I saw a small rectangular flat piece of rusty metal which I asked for and he gave me as a gift. It is the musical note bar of a harmonica. The rest of the instrument has been burned away, and we will never know whose lips were upon it or the songs it played, but I will forever choose to hear in my mind the happy sound of singing children, too innocent for such death, rather than the screams of their final agony. Mel doesn't have that privilege. He must keep his promise to never forget.

I shared a copy of the letter one evening with David Levinson, whose eyes filled with tears as he finished reading. I later helped him with the last thing he ever wrote—his holographic will. David died May 30, 2000.

Now, well beyond the seventy-fourth milestone of my life, I look back at the many side roads I have traveled. I marvel at some of the trips and wonder if others were worth the effort. All in all, I believe duty is fulfilled in the undertaking of an ordeal and not whether the initial objective is ever reached. The more difficult routes often lead to unforeseen solutions and amazing discoveries; sometimes the ultimate destination remains over the horizon.

In the Holocaust Case, making full use of the resources available in a free society, we were able to focus the media and the law on a dangerous situation and reduce the threat. The danger was not eliminated, however, and Holocaust denial remains coiled like a snake, ready to strike out with its fangs and inject its venomous and false doctrines of racial, religious, and cultural superiority.

The truth is the truth—babies and small children were deliberately exterminated in the Holocaust, and genocide and wars that treat the lives of children as collateral damage continue to take place around the world. These are indelible crimes written in the annals of humanity. They can never be erased or forgotten if we are to ever repent of the sins of war and receive absolution for the murders we seek to justify for its sake.

Over the years, I have often been urged to write about my cases, including this one. I have always felt these matters were my clients' stories, not mine; however, as genocide continues to occur around the world in places like Cambodia, Rwanda, Bosnia, Indonesia, Darfur, and the Congo, I decided to prepare this brief memoir about the horrors of a mass murder based on race, religion, and culture and the efforts to cover it up and pretend it never happened.

Looking back through the dusty and yellowed case files stored in the garage and reading what I had long suppressed and forgotten, I was forced to remember the battles and was reminded of why I undertook the mission.

I once again write for the Children of the Holocaust and now for all of the Children of Mindkind, who shall inherit the world, such as it is, when we leave them.

APPENDICES

The following material includes the Declaration Regarding Urgency of Proceedings filed in support of our Request for Priority, Willis Carto's responsive declaration, excerpts from the arguments made during the hearing and the court's ruling, the Motion on Judicial Notice, and a Memorandum Regarding Corporate Liability.

Also included are several documents from Carto's Washington, DC lawsuit against me, including my Rule 11 and Rule 12(b) motions and declarations. Also, Carto attached my Declaration Regarding Urgency of Proceedings to his complaint in the Washington lawsuit. One paragraph of the declaration has been omitted out of fairness and an abundance of caution, as it contained information that may have been the subject of other lawsuits by Willis Carto. A similar paragraph in Appendix E has also been omitted.

Except for minor typography, punctuation, and spelling differences, these documents are copies of those found in the official files of *Mermelstein vs. Institute for Historical Review, et al*, Case Number C 356 542 of the Superior Court of the State of California for the County of Los Angeles and *Willis A. Carto, Plaintiff, vs. William J. Cox, et al., Defendants*, Civil Action number 83-1788 of the United States District Court for the District of Columbia. As such, they are historical documents of public interest.

(A) Declaration Regarding Urgency of Proceedings

I, William Cox, declare:

That I am counsel of record for the Plaintiff in the above-entitled action.

That this case is set for motions on summary judgment on August 26, 1981.

That it has become a matter of urgency that this case proceed without delay to a prompt and just resolution of all legal issues raised in the accompanying motions.

That I am informed and believe, and upon such information and belief, do hereby declare what follows to be a true and correct summary of this case to the best of my knowledge.

The money trees of which Willis Allison Carto is the creator and proprietor constitute a deep but not impenetrable forest, at the center of which is the tangled underbrush of a secret American Nazism. That Nazism, like Carto himself, does not show its face, and hopes not to until it can show its fist.

On the edges of Carto's forest are the trees the public sees:

- The Institute for Historical Review, the Noontide Press and Independence House (all three twined together and growing out of the Legion for the Survival of Freedom).
- Liberty Lifeline (which started life as the Council on Dangerous Drugs).
- A weekly tabloid called The Spotlight.
- A radio program.
- The *Washington Observer* newsletter.
- United Republicans of America (which is not a Republican Party organization but is, rather, aimed at a takeover of the Republican Party).
- Americans for National Security.
- Save Our Schools (a group opposing public school desegregation).
- Friends of Rhodesian Independence.
- The American Southern Africa Council.
- National Youth Alliance, the successor organization to Youth for Wallace, a campaign organization formed

through Carto's Action Associates for George Wallace's 1968 attempt to gain the presidency.

Deep in the forest is an ugly tangle of Nazism and racism, of which the most public manifestation has been the publication of the *American Mercury*, once a proud journal of literature and opinion and now a blatantly racist and anti-Semitic magazine that went through the hands of General Edwin A. Walker to Willis Carto before Carto turned it over in 1979 to Ned Touchstone, who has been on the Board of Policy of Carto's Liberty Lobby while serving as editor of the journal of the White Citizens' Councils.

The racism of the most visible Carto organizations is masked by an apparent respectability. Nowhere has Carto sought that respectability more than in the Institute for Historical Review, which with the Noontide Press and Independence House (both devoted to publishing) operate under the Legion for the Survival of Freedom out of an office in Torrance, California.

The Institute is described in its publications as "a non-profit educational foundation" established in 1978 "to investigate the positive causes and nature of war, and to disseminate those findings." Achieving white Anglo-Saxon supremacy is, for Willis Carto, a "positive" cause of war.

In the meantime, as a fundraising bulletin issued by the Institute says, "the main focus" of the organization's "research and education program has been the debunking of the so-called 'Holocaust,'" which this bulletin alleges "is continually flaunted as the main 'reason' for America's dog-like devotion to the illegal state of Israel."

On the surface, the institute's "main focus," while peculiar and abhorrent to many, is well within the areas protected by First Amendment guarantees of freedom of speech and of the press. In fact, Willis Carto has goals more far-reaching than propaganda and persuasion. The Institute is but one arm of an organized, nationwide campaign of anti-Semitism and racism that has as its ultimate objective domination by a pure "Aryan" race of all North America and all Europe under the leadership of Willis Allison Carto.

In this campaign, the plaintiff, Melvin Mermelstein, was selected as a specific target precisely because he was a survivor of the Holocaust and of the Nazi death camp at Auschwitz. In choosing him, the institute attacked a man who was extraordinarily vulnerable to anti-Semitism and, particularly, to assertions that he lied in bearing eyewitness testimony to the unspeakable cruelties of the Holocaust—cruelties that have obsessed him since he saw his mother and sisters driven into the gas chambers at Auschwitz and since he discovered that he alone of his family had escaped Nazi oppression alive.

Whatever right Willis Carto has to lie about the Holocaust, he cannot with impunity turn the lie into a dagger aimed at the heart of a Holocaust victim whose psychological vulnerability is intense and deep.

How Willis Carto and his agents came to aim this dagger at this man is a story that began with Carto's first political activities in the mid-1950s in San Francisco, where Carto had been working as a debt collector for Household Finance Corporation. He became a Director of the Libertarian Congress of Freedom and executive secretary of an anti-Semitic organization called Liberty and Property. He formed the Joint Council for Repatriation, dedicated to the deportation of American blacks to Africa. He also formed Liberty Lobby, which is today the base of his national operations.

In 1959, he went to Belmont, Massachusetts to work for the John Birch Society, an organization he left in less than a year after a dispute with its founder, Robert Welch. Returning to California, Carto centered his efforts on fundraising for Liberty Lobby. In January 1961, he published the first Liberty Letter. It was the ancestor of Carto's current major publication, *The Spotlight*, a weekly 36-page tabloid with a staff of 25 and a paid circulation of 300,000.

Carto's book-publishing operations, conducted under the corporate umbrella of the Legion for the Survival of Freedom, are undertaken by Independence House and the Noontide Press. Independence House publishes one book and one book only: *A Manual on How to Establish a Trust and Reduce Taxation*, by Martin A. Larson. The price: $195. Liberty Lifeline Foundation, a Carto operation in Los Angeles, provides tax and estate planning in setting up trusts under conditions where all or part of the proceeds are ultimately paid to Liberty Lobby.

The foundation was incorporated as a nonprofit corporation in August 1969, as the Council on Dangerous Drugs with Richard Norton, Anthony Hilder and Kenneth Waite as its board of directors. In October 1978, the name—but not the stated purpose—was changed at a corporate meeting. Ann Cinquina became the chairman and LaVonne Furr became the secretary. Elisabeth Carto is the treasurer.

The Noontide Press is primarily a book publisher, although it has issued a 25-cent flier called "The White Student," which promotes

Noontide Press books and includes a fictitious "interview" with an unnamed "physical anthropologist from a leading university." The "anthropologist" identifies blacks as mentally inferior to whites. "Have you ever heard of Auschwitz?" a fictional "Mr. Gallstein" asks him. "Do you know what this kind of thinking can lead to? They made eight million of my people into lampshades and soap. The soap came in three scents and the cakes were shaped like swastikas. I'll bet you'd never heard that before."

"Yes, more or less," the "anthropologist" replies. "But I thought the official total was six million."

The anti-black, anti-Semitic theme of "The White Student" runs through the Noontide Press books. Noontide Press and Independence House, operating through the Legion for the Survival of Freedom, have a stock of 100,000 "racial survival" books with such titles as *The Inequality of the Races*; *Teutonic Unity*; *Our Nordic Race*; *White Man, Think Again*; and *Imperium*.

In 1965 or 1966, Carto became an officer of the Legion for the Survival of Freedom, a Texas corporation whose officers in February 1965 were Mrs. Marcia J. Hoyt, president; Mrs. LaVonne Furr, vice president; and Edwin A. Walker, secretary-treasurer. Before a merger move with another Carto organization, the Committee for Religious Development, Inc. of Washington, DC, General Edwin Walker was displaced as a Legion officer. With the merger, control of a Legion publication, the *American Mercury,* passed to Carto.

Under Carto's guidance the *American Mercury*, founded in 1924 by Henry Louis Mencken and George Jean Nathan and once famed as a leader in American thought and in finding and publishing new writers of distinction, was turned into a thoroughly scruffy fascist and anti-Semitic magazine that was sold in dual subscriptions with another Carto publication, a newsletter called *Washington Observer*.

As he expanded his publishing efforts, Carto also began to form the organizations through which he operates today. These organizations on the edges of Carto's forest are designed to reach Americans with specialized interests and to provide fronts for activities that might be suspect if carried out under the direct aegis of Liberty Lobby.

The money trees are luxuriant and green. Willis Carto's direct mail and radio fund-raising, supplemented by an astonishing ten and a half million copy sale in 1964 of *LBJ: A Political Biography*, enabled Carto's Liberty Lobby to acquire for his Washington operations a 30-room building on the corner of Independence Avenue and Third Street in the capital.

The Lyndon Johnson "biography" was not Carto's first book-publishing labor of hate. An earlier and far more important one provides the key to Carto's racial and political views and to his quest for power. That book—one of the "racial survival" publications of the Noontide Press—is *Imperium: The Philosophy of History and Politics*. It was first published in the United States in 1962 under the imprint of a right-wing magazine called *Truthseeker*. Subsequent editions have been published by the Noontide Press. *Imperium* is an American *Mein Kampf*.

Its author, Francis Parker Yockey, was an honor student in high school in Chicago and was graduated *cum laude* from the Notre Dame University School of Law. During service in the US Army in the early years of World War II, Yockey became deeply disturbed. He went AWOL, was returned, examined by psychiatrists, and given a medical discharge on the ground that he suffered from "dementia praecox, paranoid type."

In late 1945, Yockey took a job doing legal research for the War Crimes Tribunal in Wiesbaden, Germany. He quit after eleven months because of what he felt was the commission's unfair treatment of the Nazi leaders. After returning briefly to the United States, he went to Brittas Bay, Ireland. In that remote setting on the Irish Bay, he wrote *Imperium*, the testament of hate that became Willis Carto's bible.

Its intellectual ancestry is the writing of three men: Oswald Spengler, Friedrich Nietzsche and Alfred Rosenberg, the Estonian who joined Hitler in 1919, edited the Nazi party newspaper, and provided the anti-Semitic and anti-Christian philosophical underpinning for Hitler's drive for power.

The dedication of *Imperium*—"To the hero of the Second World War"—is enigmatic when a reader first sees it. The book itself makes it clear that Yockey's hero is Adolf Hitler, whom Yockey sees as the leader of the racially pure "High Culture." *Imperium* defines "the final life-task of the Culture" as "the subjection of its known world to its domination"—a goal slightly more ambitious than that proposed by Rosenberg in *Der Mythus des 20. Jahrhunderts* (*The Myth of the 20th Century*), which argued that as representatives of the "Nordic race" Germans were entitled to dominate Europe.

Yockey, like Carto, declared that Hitler and Germany failed in their historic mission because of the Jews. Yockey suggested, also like Carto, that with a new hero, a Hitler reborn, an American majority can be forged to triumph where Hitler failed. America, *Imperium* announces, has "a bare majority that is indisputably American racially, spiritually, nationally."

"The other half," the *Imperium* reader is told, "consists of Negroes, Jews, unassimilated Southeastern Europeans, Mexicans, Chinese, Siamese, Levantines, Slavs, and Indians."

To this bigot's fantasy, Willis Allison Carto furnished an awestruck introduction. In its 35 pages he calls *Imperium* "prophetic; the work of an intuitive seer," and, demanding "a racial view of history," proclaims that "the genetic interpretation of race is a necessary, useful and valid one if we are to see all of our problems clearly and accurately."

It is all simple. Jews are the "Culture Distorter." And "Negro equality is easier to believe in if there are no Negroes around to destroy the concept." True Europeans and Americans are Aryans with a civilization whose origins were not in the Middle East with Jews and Christians but in Europe itself. The evidence is clear: "The world wears leather shoes and trousers, not sandals and togas. Wearing apparel very similar to items sold at Sears, Roebuck today have (sic) been discovered in Europe dating back some three thousand years."

In Yockey's disturbed mind, his book was "only in form a book at all." It was "in reality . . . a part of the life of *action*" and "a turning point in European history, a late turning-point but a real one."

Willis Carto accepted that. He suggested in his introduction to *Imperium*, that his publication of the book was, perhaps, "in itself, concrete evidence that its prophecy is being worked out." With the writing and publication of *Imperium*, he exulted, "now, for the first time, those soldiers who enlist in the service of the West have a profound theory to inspire and guide them."

Guided by that "profound theory," Carto calls for a single-minded and intolerant power which can clean and redeem our fast-decaying, rotting milieu," and declares:

> . . . although our job is to *rebuild* we must not lose sight of the reality, for we cannot rebuild until we have *captured*. Political power is the essential criterion . . . and to the goal of political power all else must be temporarily sacrificed . . . Those who would guide the West back across the Styx and out of the dark must

travel first through the gates of Hell. (emphasis in original)

In June 1960, in his underwear with his Nazi boots on, Francis Parker Yockey died by his own hand, of potassium cyanide poisoning, in the San Francisco jail where he was being held on passport violation charges. Shortly before, Willis Carto had paid him a visit. "I knew," Carto wrote later, "that I was in the presence of a great force, and I could feel History standing aside me."

Carto's choice of associates in Liberty Lobby underscored his aim of giving political reality to Yockey's thesis that in the United States the "High Culture" could accomplish the "final life-task" of subjecting "its known world to its domination." Among those Carto added to the Board of Policy of Liberty Lobby in 1964 were Ned Touchstone, editor of *The Councilor*, the journal of the White Citizens' Councils; Tyler Kent, convicted by a British court in 1940 of divulging secrets to the Axis while he was an employee at the American Embassy in London; and Ed Delaney, an American who broadcast over Berlin Radio during the Hitler regime.

[Omission of paragraph]

If Liberty Lobby is the base of Carto's operations, the Institute for Historical Review and the Legion for the Survival of Freedom are its heart. These are the organizations directly dedicated to clearing Hitler's name and persuading Americans that Francis Parker Yockey was right, and the world wrong, about the Nazi genocide of European Jews. There was no genocide, Yockey wrote—only propaganda. As Yockey tells it:

> The propaganda was technically quite complete. "Photographs" were supplied in millions of copies. Thousands of the people who had been killed published accounts of their experiences in these camps. Hundreds of thousands more made fortunes in postwar black-markets. "Gas-chambers" that did not exist were photographed, and a "gasmobile" was invented to titillate the mechanically-minded.

That is the message of the institute's Journal of Historical Review and of the "Revisionist Convention" conducted by the Institute each year with the intention of revising history to erase the Holocaust from its pages. It was the message of a "reward" offered by the Institute at the 1979 convention: $50,000 to anyone who could prove that Jews were killed in gas chambers at Auschwitz.

This bizarre "reward" offer was proposed by Anthony Hilder, a director of the Liberty Lifeline Foundation. Carto urged William David McCalden, who, under the name of Lewis Brandon, had been chosen by Carto and LaVonne Furr as director of the Institute for Historical Review, to consult Hilder, a public relations consultant, at Hilder's office in Hollywood. McCalden told Carto about Hilder's suggestion of a reward for proof the Holocaust occurred. Carto embraced the idea and told McCalden the "reward" offer would be announced in a press conference after the 1979 "Revisionist Convention."

Carto and McCalden did not discuss what funds would be used to pay the "reward" should anyone win it. "It was never really a question," McCalden said in a deposition taken June 12, 1981 on behalf of the plaintiff.

The "reward" offer was designed to arouse doubt about the killing of Jews in the Holocaust. It was calculated to suggest that what was common knowledge—through newspaper accounts, photographs, books, films, government documents (including Nazi documents) and other sources—was in fact nothing but a mass delusion contrived by a Jewish conspiracy.

If Americans could accept that, they could be persuaded of the truth of Yockey's assertion that the Jews were "the real victor" in the Second World War, and that in the victory of the Jews "the American armies were just as completely defeated as the armies from the mother-soil of the Culture." Americans would then be ready to follow Willis A. Carto "across the Styx and out of the dark." But before they reached that world free of Jews, they would, as Carto said, "travel first through the gates of Hell."

For all of Carto's expertise in peddling hate and fear by mail, in raising funds and building an underground organization dedicated to a renascence of Nazism, there is no evidence that Willis Carto could lead a civilized nation into anti-Semitic and anti-Black lunacy. There is no evidence that he could persuade Americans by the millions to follow him in an Aryan purity crusade through the gates of Hell to achieve a world that recognized the ancient ancestry of the Sears Roebuck suit. But there was no evidence that Adolf Hitler, starting with a few followers in 1919, could by the 1930s transform his tiny Nationalsozialistische Deutsche Arbeiterpartel (National Socialist Workers' Party), through his skills as an organizer and fund-raiser, into a movement that turned the German nation against the Jews—a people who constituted less than one percent of the German population, who had intermarried with German Christians, who were leaders in science and the arts, and who were in lifestyle and loyalty to Germany no different from the other 99 percent. And yet Hitler, who like Yockey and like Carto was a lonely man who lived in a fantasy world, made anti-Semitism the focus of this successful campaign for power in Germany and, once he had attained that power, the focus of his terrible genocidal exercise of it.

When Alfred Rosenberg enunciated the Master Race theories he eventually turned into *The Myth of the 20th Century*, he found few adherents outside Hitler's immediate circle. When Arthur Butz wrote, and the Institute for Historical Review published, *The Hoax of the 20th Century*, he found few adherents outside the crypto-Nazis of Carto's immediate circle. But ripples spread and circles grow, and in the end a civilization can be engulfed.

The first ripples from the "reward" offer made by Carto's Institute for Historical Review were mightily pleasing to those who threw the stone. "We have now generated more publicity for the Revisionist case than any other movement since World War Two," Brandon/McCalden declared in a letter to subscribers to the Journal of Historical Review. He added:

> Today, we measure our publicity in vertical inches of piles of newspaper clippings!
>
> Most of the publicity has been excellent. True, there have been a few misquotes and extrapolations here and there. But by and large we are extremely pleased. Recently, we even had fairly objective coverage in the most important papers in this country, the *New York Times* (11 March 1981) and the *Washington Post* (11 April 1981) . . . We have also been on the air on phone-in radio programs all around the country. Requests for TV interviews have come in, not just from Los Angeles stations, but even from networked shows in New York.

This initial publicity, however gratifying to those who had sought it, quickly stilled. There were no signs that Americans were ready to follow Willis Carto through the gates of Hell, or that Jews were willing to dignify his schemes by responding to his "reward" offer. With only a few exceptions, letters to the editor scoffed at Carto's thesis. Some treated it as ridiculous. A few were outraged.

Among the latter was Melvin Mermelstein, who knew the gates of Hell that waited if Carto could first persuade millions that Hitler's deeds were fiction and could then turn Yockey's fantasy into deeds. Mermelstein wrote letters to the *Press-Telegram,* a daily newspaper published in Long Beach, California; to *Jewish Heritage,* a weekly newspaper published in Los Angeles; and to The *Jerusalem Post,* an internationally circulated English-language daily newspaper published in Israel. All three published Mermelstein's letter. The publication in *The Jerusalem Post* brought swift responses from Carto's "Liberty" empire employees and associates.

One response, an "Open Letter to a Racist and Exterminationist," was widely circulated to Jews as well as to others. In it, Ditlieb Felderer, a member of the Editorial Advisory Committee of the *Journal for Historical Review,* accused Mermelstein of "peddling the extermination hoax," and of surviving the Holocaust through "pecuniary stealth" and through collaboration with the Nazis. Since Felderer, Carto, and their associates contend in the *Journal for Historical Review* that no Jews were murdered by the Nazis, it is clear that this letter's infamous lies could only have been contrived to damage Mermelstein's reputation and to inflict the most grievous personal wounds. Mermelstein separated from his father and brother at Auschwitz at his father's bidding. To suggest that the separation that saved his life was collaboration with the Nazis who killed his mother and sisters, and who almost certainly killed his father and brother, was to strike Mel Mermelstein at the most vulnerable, the most easily penetrated part of his personal armor. It was a sadistic stroke worthy of the first Nazis, the men Willis Carto admires most.

A second response to Mermelstein's letter came from the Institute for Historical Review. It was signed "Lewis Brandon," a fictitious name that has been used by Willis Carto and by David McCalden, then director of the Institute. (The use of fictitious names by Carto and McCalden did not begin with this letter. McCalden has used the names Julius Finkelstein and David Findelstein. Carto has a list of fictitious names worthy of the late W. C. Fields: Lee Roberts, Asgard Hall, George Jenkins, Merlin Featherstone, Jay Bruce MacLeod, Keith K. Kenyon, and E. L. Anderson, PhD.)

The letter from "Lewis Brandon" and the Institute for Historical Review, dated November 20, 1980, challenged Mermelstein to apply for the $50,000 "reward." An application form was enclosed. The letter concluded:

If we do not hear from you, we will be obliged to draw our own conclusions and publicize this fact to the mass media, including the *Jerusalem Post*.

I look forward to hearing from you very soon.

"Lewis Brandon" thus made it imperative that Melvin Mermelstein close the circle and bring together in confrontation two men, each then 54 years old, who had been profoundly affected by Adolf Hitler's determination to rid the world of Jews. Mel Mermelstein, who had been its victim, and Willis Carto, who has dedicated his life to making it a reality.

Mermelstein accepted the challenge. Through counsel, William Cox, on December 18, 1980, less than a month after he received the taunting letter from the Institute for Historical Review, a letter went to "Lewis Brandon." The letter said that Mermelstein "fully accepts your offer" and "assumes that the sufficiency of his evidence will be judged by an impartial fact finder, that all proceedings will be open to public and media observation, and that the matter will be resolved in a timely manner."

The letter cautioned that "if no response is had by January 20, 1981, civil proceedings to enforce the contract will be instituted . . ." The letter was accompanied by a notarized declaration by Mermelstein of his experiences at Auschwitz, by an additional offer of proof that named other eyewitnesses and scientific witnesses and identifies physical evidence that would be available for the tribunal judging the matter, and by the filled-out application that had been supplied with the Institute's letter of November 20, 1980.

A letter to Mermelstein dated January 20, 1981 and signed Lewis Brandon declared: "I am still deliberating on your proposal with our Committee members and will get back to you just as soon as we have arrived at some concrete decisions."

In a later deposition, William David McCalden said he wrote that letter after conferring only with Willis Carto.

On January 26, 1981, a letter from William Cox, counsel for plaintiff, went to Brandon. It said:

Your letter dated January 20, 1981, has been received and discussed with Mr. Mermelstein.

We continue to consider a speedy resolution of this matter quite important in that it is the honor of Mr. Mermelstein that is daily put in question by your delay.

Therefore, unless you perform in accordance with the contract in which you have now entered by February 6, 1981, we shall be forced to file an action in the Superior Court to enforce his rights.

On January 27, 1981, in a letter to William Cox as attorney for Melvin Mermelstein, Lewis Brandon wrote:

I have now discussed your client's claim with my colleagues.

We also had another claim from Mr. Simon Wiesenthal. He wishes to claim the $50,000 for proof of the gassings and the $25,000 for proof that Anne Frank's Diary is authentic. He declined to claim the $25,000 for proof that Jews were turned into soap.

In the circumstances, we have decided to deal with Mr. Wiesenthal's claim for the Anne Frank Diary authenticity, and then deal simultaneously with both his and your client's claim for the $50,000 later . . .

Thereafter, all in the present year, 1981, the following events occurred in sequence:

February 19—Melvin Mermelstein filed lawsuit C 356542 against the Institute for Historical Review, et al.

March 17—Lewis Brandon/David McCalden was personally served with a summons and a copy of the complaint in the lawsuit.

March 20—A letter from the Institute to William Cox proposed that Mermelstein's evidence be considered at the Institute's "Revisionist Convention" November 20-23 at the University of California's Lake Arrowhead Conference Center.

March 31—A letter to the Institute from Cox noted that the Institute had apparently expanded the proof desired from Mermelstein to include evidence that gassing of Jews was an official policy. The letter also noted that when the summons and complaint were served on March 17 to a person who acknowledged himself to be David McCalden, that person "refused to acknowledge himself to be 'Lewis Brandon.'" The letter added: "I must ascertain with some greater degree of certainty who it is with whom I correspond . . . If your answer is not filed with the Superior Court by April 17, 1981, I intend to take action to receive default judgment on the proceedings."

April 16—A letter from "Lewis Brandon" to subscribers to the Institute for Historical Review described the $50,000 "reward" offer as "our No. 1 gimmick," and declared further:

> The reward was a gimmick to attract publicity; and it was a gimmick that worked! All we needed was some naive zealot to walk into our trap . . . I must now tell you that on 9 April 1981 I wrote to the Committee of the Legion for the Survival of Freedom (IHR's "holding company") to advise them that I wished to resign at the end of April. My resignation was regretfully tendered and it was regretfully received. I am standing down because I wish to direct myself into other fields; other areas which are in need of review.

May 18—University of California President David Saxon denied the Institute for Historical Review permission to use the university's Lake Arrowhead Conference Center for the "Revisionist Convention" scheduled to take place November 20-23. Dr. Saxon cited a "pattern of deception" in cancelling the institute's reservations for the conference center. Dean Keith Sexton of the university extension program said in a statement made available to the press that the Institute director had used a false name in applying to rent the university facilities, had been unavailable for further contact with university officials and had admitted that the "reward" for proof of the Holocaust was "a publicity gimmick."

May 20 —Thomas James Marcellus, Brandon/McCalden's successor as director of the Institute or Historical Review, gave a deposition, taken on behalf of the plaintiff in this action. In that deposition he was asked these questions and gave these answers:

> Q. Who will be the experts that you would assemble to hear additional evidence? In other words, if you had to put on a conference and to assemble a group of people to hear the reward offer or acceptance, who would be on that list?

> A. Well, we might have Dr. Faurisson, who is a documents expert. We might have Felderer, who has spent considerable amount of time in Auschwitz and Auschwitz-Birkenau. And we might have Dr. Butz, who has done a fantastic amount of research, too, on the population figures and that sort of thing.

> Q. And anyone else?

> A. At the moment, I think it would be those three.

All three are members of the Editorial Advisory Board of the *Journal of Historical Review*. Robert Faurisson, a French national, was convicted in France of libel for denying the fact of the Holocaust, was put on probation, fined and ordered to pay damages. Ditlieb Felderer, a Swedish national, publishes the anti-Semitic *Jewish Information Bulletin* and is under investigation by the national police of Sweden for comments made in that publication about the Mermelstein lawsuit. Arthur Butz is the author of *The Hoax of the 20th Century*, a Noontide Press book that contends that there was no Holocaust.

He is not a historian, and the thesis of his book has been repudiated by the president of the university at which he teaches.

June 11—A letter from Richard Fusilier, counsel for defendants, to William Cox as counsel for plaintiff renewed the proposal that Mermelstein's evidence be considered at the November Revisionist Convention and declared, in part:

> This evidence must be presented to a designated panel assembled by the Institute.
>
> The panel will consist of individuals selected by the Institute on the basis of their integrity and probity.
>
> If your client should find the panel's decision to be objectionable then that will be a proper time for him to sue . . .

This letter demanded an acceptance of these conditions by June 15. Since the lawsuit was already under way, the letter deserved—and received—no response.

July 13—An article headlined "Exterminationist Refuses Offer" was published in Carto's weekly newspaper, *The Spotlight*. This article alleged, falsely, that "Mel Mermelstein, peripatetic Holocaust 'witness,' has refused a continuing offer by the Institute for Historical Review (IHR) to consider his claim for the $50,000 reward offered by the Institute to the first person who can prove that Jews were gassed in gas chambers at Auschwitz." The article further alleged, falsely, that Mermelstein "launched a publicity blitz under the guise of a $17 million lawsuit."

In fact, it was the Institute for Historical Review that had, having pressed Melvin Mermelstein for a quick acceptance of its challenge, refused to give Mermelstein's application timely consideration. It was the institute whose director declared that the "reward offer" was a "publicity gimmick." But having engineered a confrontation that was to plunge Mermelstein into deep mental anguish, having aimed the dagger of a lie at his victim's heart, Willis Allison Carto used the most widely circulated of his publications and another lie to twist the dagger.

Melvin Mermelstein resisted. He feels an obligation to resist. The necessity of such resistance is suggested in *The Informed Heart*, a book in which Dr. Bruno Bettelheim, himself a former Nazi concentration camp prisoner, discusses that experience and the psychology of its perpetrators and victims. Dr. Bettelheim writes:

> At the time of the first boycott of Jewish stores the whole external goal of the Nazis was the possessions of the Jews. They even let Jews take some of them out of the country if they would just go, leaving the bulk of their possessions behind. For a long time the intention of the Nazis, and of their first discriminatory laws, was to force undesirable minorities, including Jews, into emigration. Only when this did not work was the extermination policy instituted, though it also followed the logic of the Nazi racial ideology. But one wonders if the notion that millions of Jews (and later foreign nationals) would submit to extermination did not also result from seeing how much degradation they would accept without fighting back. The persecution of the Jews worsened, slow step by slow step, when no violent resistance occurred. It may have been Jewish acceptance, without fight, of ever harsher discrimination and degradation that first gave the SS the idea that they could be gotten to the point where they would walk to the gas chambers on their own.

The continuing story of Melvin Mermelstein's refusal to walk to the gas chambers on his own began seventeen years after he was born in Mugaczewe, Czechoslovakia, in 1926—the same year Willis Allison Carto was born in Fort Wayne, Indiana.

Both men have lived their lives in the shadow of Adolf Hitler's racial theories, and their confrontation in this courtroom is, for both, colored by those theories.

For Melvin Mermelstein, those theories gave birth to a nightmare that deprived him first of liberty and then his family. He was interned with his mother, father, brother, and two sisters at Auschwitz-Birkenau. He saw his mother and sisters forced into the gas chambers there. He does not know the fate of his father and brother, but he knows what his father said to him as he pointed to the flaming chimneys of the gas ovens and they parted for the last time: "If we're apart, I won't see your suffering and you won't see mine—and to see that would be the greatest suffering of all."

This nightmare has dominated Mel Mermelstein's life. "It never leaves me," he wrote in *By Bread Alone: The Story of A-4685.* "It never recedes into the past. It never fades away, but only urges me on. It spends my money and it collects books on the Holocaust, which line my shelves at home. It collects hundreds of photos of the past, and snaps new ones of the places that still dot the old battlefields, the ghettos and the death camps. It drives me to write scores of letters, pushes me into lecture halls. It guides my pen. It remains the master, and I have no choice but to do its bidding."

For Willis Allison Carto, Hitler's Master Race theories have been a dream that has made his money and guided his career as a writer, promoter and creator of a multimillion-dollar business empire. "Hitler's defeat," he has written, "was the defeat of Europe. And America. How could we have been so blind? The blame, it seems, must be laid at the door of the international Jews. It was their propaganda, lies and demands which blinded the West as to what Germany was doing."

"The revolutionists have seen to it," Carto has declared, "that only a few Americans are concerned about the inevitable niggerfication of America." It is Willis Carto's self-decreed mission to multiply into a majority the number of Americans who share that Hitlerian concern. He has carried out that mission conspiratorially, secretly, single mindedly, skillfully—at great cost to our democratic society and with immense financial rewards to himself and the organizations he leads and inspires.

Willis Carto leads organized anti-Semitism in the United States. His dream is to succeed the Fuehrer as savior of the "Aryan race" in America and Europe.

In pursuit of that goal, he has begun, as Hitler did, with the establishment of an organization that preaches national unity but practices divisiveness and hate. Carto presides over a network of corporations and publications devoted to a long-term process of persuading Americans of the validity of Hitlerian racial theories as espoused in Francis Parker Yockey's *Imperium.*

In the initial states of that process, Carto's Legion for the Survival of Freedom, working through the Institute for Historical Review, selected its first specific American Jewish victim: Melvin Mermelstein.

Because Mermelstein had narrowly escaped being one of the last Jewish victims of Adolf Hitler, Yockey, and Carto's "hero of the Second World War," he was from the Institute's viewpoint an especially apt victim. Because he is a Holocaust victim whose life has been dedicated to preventing a repetition of that saddest chapter in the history of mankind, Mermelstein is, from his viewpoint, an especially apt adversary. The damage he has suffered has been great: depression and extreme mental anguish. His victory will belong not only to him but to all free men and women, and to his mother, father, brother, and sisters and the others murdered in the Holocaust Willis Carto denies and wishes to repeat.

A "Reward" offer that started as a "publicity gimmick" became a weapon for Willis Carto and a matter of honor for Melvin Mermelstein. The weapon continues to function so long as resolution of this dispute is delayed. While there are delays, Mermelstein is likely to suffer continued depression that will cause continuing damage to his family relationships and to his ability to perform effectively at his business. A swift adjudication of the matters at issue would enable him to resume the peaceful, secure life that was interrupted by the challenge from the Institute for Historical Review.

DATED: August 10, 1981

WILLIAM COX, Attorney for the Plaintiff

(B) Declaration of Willis A. Carto

I, Willis A. Carto Declares:

1. Within the confines of time and space available, it is impossible for me to address all of the charges made against me by the counsel for the plaintiff. But as a matter of simple proof that his charges are maliciously untrue, irresponsible, unprofessional, designed to injure my reputation, hold me to ridicule, deny me my civil rights including freedom of speech and to put my life in danger I cite the simple fact that one of the documents he has entered as "evidence" against me—a copy of an article which appeared in *True* magazine (Nov. 1969 issue)—was the subject of a libel action which Liberty Lobby and I won. Our complaint, filed in the District Court of Oklahoma County, Oklahoma, listed 29 malicious lies in that article. The publisher, Fawcett, agreed to its liability and paid us a very satisfactory sum of money, agreed to print a factual article according to our specifications and to supply us with 50,000 free reprints of said article.

2. My philosophical and political views are well-known to anyone who is interested in them. All one has to do is to read the lengthy introduction I wrote to the book, *Imperium*. I do not need prejudiced PhDs to interpret that book for me nor does anyone else intelligent enough to read it. My interpretation of the book is clearly stated in some 60 pages of introductory material and I am proud to say that if I were to rewrite it today I would change nothing and could only add comments on how the intervening 20 years have proven the validity of what I wrote then, controversial or not. The intellectual capacity of the PhD Mr. Cox commissioned to write a review of *Imperium* is indicated by her belief that the book is "racist." The book is not racist. It may be pro-German, pro-Western and controversial but even George Lincoln Rockwell criticized the author and condemned the book because it was not racist. Mr. Rockwell was the founder of the American Nazi Party. Thus, Mr. Cox and Mr. Rockwell share a dislike of *Imperium*.

3. For the past 29 years I have unswervingly dedicated my life to propagating truth within the context of traditional Americanism. I am proud to identify with the truly great men of American history who were uniformly nationalistic, pro-Constitution and populist in their outlook. During the year of 1980 I caused to be written and printed in *The Spotlight*, a weekly newspaper published by Liberty Lobby, Inc., which I serve as Treasurer, a series of twelve articles on twelve of the greatest

Americans in our history, beginning with Thomas Jefferson and culminating with Hamilton Fish. Others included Hiram Johnson of California and Robert LaFollette of Wisconsin. I wholeheartedly share with them a profound belief in neutrality and nonintervention in foreign wars, in the Constitution and government by the people and not by minority, special-interest pressure groups. Like them, I wholeheartedly mistrust privately-owned and controlled central banking and foreign influence on our government. I am responsible for distributing millions of copies of the Constitution, George Washington's Farewell Address, books describing the privately-owned Federal Reserve System, pamphlets on "How to Write Your Congressman" and numerous other wholesome and important subjects. No one, in fact, has done more than me to educate Americans as to their rights and responsibilities under the Constitution, which I revere.

4. In my research to uncover the forces that have driven this nation repeatedly into useless foreign wars from which this nation has derived not a scintilla of benefit in any way, shape or form, I have become convinced that practically everything the American people have been told to mobilize them for war has been false. I am thoroughly convinced that Franklin D. Roosevelt "lied us into war," to quote Claire Boothe Luce, and that he deliberately set up Pearl Harbor and goaded the Japanese into attack. I am likewise convinced that the subsequent war propaganda, designed to squeeze money and blood out of the American people for the benefit of the elite classes which control the country, was also false, and this includes the gruesome, ugly tale of the alleged six million (or any other number) of Jews gassed (or otherwise dispatched) by the Nazis. And I share my repugnance of the so-called "war crimes trials," beginning with Nuremberg, with many thousands of thoughtful men and women, including the late Sen. Robert A. Taft. Any attempt to prevent me from making my well-founded views known or trying to influence others is an intolerable violation of my persona, civil and constitutional rights.

5. As the founder of the Institute for Historical Review I affirm that Mr. Dittlieb [*sic*] Felderer is not and has never been an officer, employee, director or has ever held any position of responsibility within the IHR. He spoke at our convention in 1980 and has been listed, along with others, as an editorial advisor to the "Journal of Historical [*page break*] ganizations have any connection with the Institute. [*sic—omission in the original*]

6. It is manifestly clear that neither the motives of the plaintiff nor the plaintiff's counsel will withstand investigation. If Mr. Mermelstein does not wish to relive the pain of remembering his mother and sisters who were allegedly gassed then he should stop giving lectures on the subject—unless the resulting publicity and sales of his book make the effort worthwhile. And the political motivation of Mr. Cox, who obviously sees this case as his ticket for free publicity so that he may run for office again, is equally obvious. Cox has conducted this case from the beginning to get publicity, not to win and certainly not to try the issues—which is the last thing he wants. He is trying to use my body as a stepping stone to political office. He accuses me of political ambitions in order to distract from his own abuse of process for personal gain. As just one example out of many: he announced his amended suit which added Liberty Lobby and me as defendants with loud statements to the press, but he has made no attempt to serve either. And his thick file of smear data on me was issued to the press before it was filed or delivered to the attorney for the defendants.

7. If the plaintiff and his counsel were honestly interested in proving what they allege—namely, that Jews were gassed at Auschwitz—then they would have accepted the renewed offer to try the issues contained in the letter from the defendant's attorney dated June 11, 1981 and personally delivered to counsel for the plaintiff on that date. That they ignored the letter proves that their intentions are not to try and prove the issue, which is the alleged purpose of the litigation. A copy of the cited letter is attached as Exhibit "A."

8. The attorney for the plaintiff has allied himself in a criminal conspiracy with three illegal organizations: the Anti-Defamation League of B'nai B'rith (ALD), the Jewish Defense League (JDL) and the organization which orchestrates them both, the Mossad, Israel's highly efficient espionage, terrorist and action arm. Mr. Cox has sought and has received information and assistance from the ADL, and the terroristic activities of the JDL seem strangely tied in with Mr. Cox's own brand of terrorism. I attach proof of the criminal nature of the ADL: a publication by Liberty Lobby titled, "White Paper on the DL." So far, some 25,000 copies of this document have been distributed and it has been reprinted in *The Spotlight*, with 325, 000 paid subscribers and a readership of one million. *The Spotlight* has authoritatively branded the ADL an illegally unregistered foreign agent many times. No legal action from the ADL in response to this accusation has ever been made, nor is any expected. As

for the JDL, there seems little question that it is also a foreign agent operating under the control of a foreign government. The JDL commonly conducts its demonstrations while marching around a large Israeli flag (a fact always omitted by newspaper photos of the demonstrations) and the members of the JDL describe themselves as soldiers in Israeli service. That the Department of Justice and the investigating committees of the House of Representative and the Senate of the United States fear to investigate the foreign connections of these groups and indict them for felony violation of American law is a shameful affront to American nationality and every patriotic American. A copy of the cited white paper is attached as Exhibit "B."

9. Since the initiation of this lawsuit and the resulting, purposeful barrage of psychological and physical terrorism against me, consisting of not merely a propaganda campaign of pure vitriol and hate but direct physical attacks, my wife and I have suffered severely. Only hours after the counsel for the plaintiff received the letter from the former director of the Institute for Historical Review offering to reopen the terms of the $50,000 reward to anyone who could prove the existence of gas chamber in Europe, the JDL entered the condominium building where my wife and I have lived for nine years and daubed the walls of the hallway with numerous insulting, derogatory and threatening slogans, curses and the like, and I seem to have been the prime target of this alien terrorist organization ever since. My office in Washington, DC constantly and continually receives phone calls from JDL members of a vicious, obscene and threatening nature. On or about Sunday, January 11, 1981 the condominium was again the target of JDL violence—this time a firebomb attack. The office of the Institute has been picketed twice and my residence once, with JDL thugs, marching around an Israeli flag, calling for my "Death," shouting, "Kill Carto," "We want Carto dead," calling me a "Nazi," "fascist pig" and the like. I have been attacked by a mob of JDL thugs, thrown to the ground, kicked and mauled, suffered loss of blood and other injuries including loss of personal property. One of the assailants later stated that had it not been for the timely intervention of the police, they would have killed me. Due to these and many other incidents, not to mention the nervous strain and apprehension of not knowing when a bomb would be thrown through our picture window, my wife and I have had to [*page break*] neighbors (many of whom are Jewish) for many years. [*sic—omission in the original*] Since then, the office of the Institute has been firebombed and could have

been burned to the ground. Due to these incidents I must live in a state of constant preparedness, never far from a loaded pistol which I am prepared to use should any of these cowardly assassins and traitors ever show themselves. I hold Mr. Mel Mermelstein and Mr. William Cox personally responsible for these misfortunes.

10. The attorney for the plaintiff seems to have the naive belief that if I am destroyed there will be no more serious or academic inquiry into the real facts about the history of the Second World War and the supporters of Israel will have no more reason to fear that their lifeline to American dollars and defense might be severed. This is preposterous. I did not invent the theory that the so-called "Holocaust" never happened, nor have I written any books about it. Regardless of my personal fate it is absolutely certain that the truth about this gigantic lie will become better-known every hour that passes until one day it will be officially acknowledged. Hence, Mr. Cox's attempt to paint me as uniquely evil and the one responsible for the growing doubts about the "Holocaust" is doomed to fail even if he is successful in destroying me personally.

I declare, under penalty of perjury, that the foregoing is true and correct to the best of my knowledge and belief.

Executed in Los Angeles, California, this 22nd day of August, 1981

WILLIS A. CARTO

(C) Reporter's Transcript of Hearing

Friday, October 9, 1981

APPEARANCES:

For the Plaintiff: William Cox, Esq.

For the Defendants: Richard Fusilier, Esq.

THE COURT: Now, just commenting on the obvious, I would say that this is a matter of interest to a number of people. And the television people have chosen to be here and to participate. And they have asked the clerk and the clerk has asked me to ask you gentlemen when you are speaking to go to the podium since that, apparently, is where they can function best. So if you will, please, keep that in mind.

There are a number of motions before the Court this morning. And the Court has read and considered all of the documents that you all have filed with respect to those motions both in support and in opposition.

A motion or a request for priority is off calendar as moot.

We have a request for the taking of judicial notice. And perhaps it would be well to address those requests first.

. . .

I am going to be interested in argument from you all as to the plaintiff's request that the Court take judicial notice of the fact that Jews were gassed to death at Auschwitz Concentration Camp in Poland during the summer of 1944.

. . .

THE COURT: Do you wish to be heard on your request for judicial notice?

MR. COX: Yes, your Honor. I do.

Your Honor has mentioned, firstly, Evidence Code Section 451. And as I generally understand the law relating to judicial notice—and to try to, as best I can, put that into the context of this case—obviously, from the beginning from the drafting of the complaint there was mention therein about facts that the Court could take judicial notice of.

In this particular case we are dealing with a significant historical event. If we are to place any credence in the declarations by the historians that are attached to plaintiff's moving papers, we have to recognize that the question today among reputable historians is not whether or not the event occurred, but rather, an analysis of why it occurred and what it means to us today.

Particularly, looking at 451, the idea is whether or not there is a fact, whether or not it is within generalized knowledge, whether or not it is universally known, and, particularly whether or not there is any reasonable dispute.

This is somehow seemingly, to me, the precise kind of case where it is incumbent upon the Court to take judicial notice. I point that out in our moving papers. And I think I can argue generally relating to this.

There have been many trials on this issue beginning with the Nuremberg trials following World War II.

Since that time there have been at least three very large general trials in Germany relating to this. One is the trial of the so-called industrialists.

The other is the Auschwitz trials that were conducted relating to various personnel who were assigned there.

And then, lastly, recently, certain trials ended. And, particularly, the trial of Adolf Eichmann in Israel.

During none of these trials was there ever a denial of the fact that, one, there was an extermination program.

Secondly, whether or not that Jews were gassed or that gas was used to kill Jews in Auschwitz.

So what we have here today is a situation where if the Court is to say to the plaintiff that this is something that you have to prove as an element of your case or that this is an issue in your case, then we are in that position of the prosecutors in perhaps the Auschwitz trials, in the trial of Eichmann in Israel. And that is that that would require the production of a tremendous amount of evidence, perhaps so great in order to properly prepare such an issue for determination that it would be simply beyond the ability of the plaintiff.

I urge that that would be the case.

THE COURT: Now, your suit here is on a contract.

MR. COX: There are a number of issues. Perhaps I can jump ahead and address that. I was going to do that next anyway.

In terms of the contract, if the Court were to view this as being a unilateral contract, that is the position of the defendants. That is not the position of the plaintiff.

If that were to be true, then we would be in that kind of a situation where we would be saying, the plaintiff would be saying, that there was full performance. Through his declaration, which was originally attached to his acceptance of the offer, that which he sent in the mail, was a signed, notarized declaration made by him which if believed—and that is the law of this state. The testimony of any one witness, if believed, is sufficient to establish any disputed fact.

If that be true, then the unilateral contract is proof under the law of reward; the Jesse James case that is cited in our moving papers.

Now, in addition, there are more causes of action alleged in this lawsuit other than contract.

Particularly directing the Court's attention to the alleged Tort No. 4, I believe, "Injurious denial of established fact," therein it is alleged that the plaintiffs—defendants—have taken a fact of history; they have twisted it around and they have used it in order to create a great lie. And they have used this great lie in a way—what they have done is they have slapped the plaintiff Mel Mermelstein in the face with this great lie. So to that extent it becomes very relevant whether or not the Holocaust occurred; whether or not it occurred in such a way as to be reasonably beyond dispute.

And I believe that is the question that we ultimately must come to hear today.

It was a very difficult task assembling the evidence—not evidence, but the information that was a duty upon me and my law firm to present to the Court in relation to this. Part of the difficulty was not in finding information to support this point, but rather in trying to wade through the incredible mound of information that is available. It is, I believe, well put forth in here the extent as best we can of that information.

The question then becomes finally whether or not it is subject to reasonable dispute. And I suggest to you that if the Court is interested, I can argue both sides. I can argue the information that we have placed before the Court and I can compare that to that which the defendants have responded with, add to that one issue —

THE COURT: No, I don't think so.

MR. FUSILIER: I'll say that what history says and what the facts are may not be the same.

Napoleon said, "What is history but a fable agreed upon?"

The crux of the situation here is they wanted someone to prove it.

We know what the politicians said. A lot of non-political people say different things. The thing is can Mr. Mermelstein prove it?

We cannot take judicial notice of a disputed fact. The contract was —

THE COURT: Excuse me. We can take judicial notice of a disputed fact.

If your lawsuit said the sun did not come up yesterday, the Court could certainly take judicial notice of that even though that was the heart of your lawsuit.

MR. FUSILIER: I agree. I am arguing—I think the Court has grasped the entire situation here. So I'll sit down on this argument, Your Honor. Thank you.

THE COURT: All right.

MR. COX: The position of the plaintiff is not that by recognizing or taking judicial notice of the existence of the fact that Jews were gassed in Auschwitz that our burden will thereby be totally relieved. That is not our position at all. It is an absolute element of one of the alleged torts that is in the complaint. And more than that, it has a tremendous amount of relevance on the first cause of action which relates to whether or not a contract occurred.

But particularly, if it is either one of two things—this is really what the plaintiff's case is all about, I suppose—either there was a Holocaust that is simply so far beyond our comprehension—I know that it is certainly beyond my ability to use language to describe what my own research and efforts in this case for almost one year now has shown.

I know only this: That is that I stand here before the Court with my own agenda and my own reasons for having taken this case and prosecuting it as best I can. And that is that throughout all of this literature, throughout all of the testimony, throughout the entire 35-year history of our awareness of what happened during World War II, in the middle of that, nowhere in any of these trials has it been denied that it occurred.

And, secondly, what even the defendants say in this particular case, they say well, this was a labor thing. People were brought there and they were selected to labor in various industrial plants.

But where did all the babies go, Your Honor? That is the question. Where did the children go? They were not subject to labor. They were not available: they were not there. And they were put to death. And that is really what this case is all about.

If that is true, then the plaintiff Mel Mermelstein at age 17 was one of the youngest that would have survived that camp. Below him and younger than him, they did not live. They were not selected to work.

He survived that and went through an experience that neither you nor I nor anyone else who has not been there can understand and appreciate. That horrible event has to be contained within his mind. And it is embodied in this entire case, both on the one hand that it did in fact happen and on the second part that it did in fact happen and it is a part of his being. It is part of what this case is all about.

To be suddenly slapped with this —

MR. FUSILIER: I would object to this, Your Honor. That is not the question, I submit, Your Honor.

THE COURT: I think I understand your point, Mr. Cox.

. . .

THE COURT: This injurious denial of an established fact to me really sounds like intentional infliction of emotional distress. I don't see it as a separate identifiable tort.

MR. COX: It is obviously not Hornbook; the reason for it being there—

THE COURT: I am a simple person. I think in simple terms.

MR. COX: It was drafted as simply as it could be put.

The creation of this cause of action in terms of its drafting came from the situation where we have this kind of conduct that does not fit squarely within defamation and the terms of it being libelous. And on the other hand it does not fit—in other words, in a minute here I'll be arguing intentional infliction of emotional distress.

THE COURT: I'll bet you are. Because if there is something here, that is what it is.

MR. COX: I won't detract from that argument.

But I do feel what we have here is a unique kind of situation because it is different.

The very magnitude of the subject of the intentional execution of such a gigantic number of persons in an extermination scheme in which the plaintiff moved through as a 17-year-old boy is such that what you truly have, it is much like—well, we compare it to yelling fire in a crowded theatre.

In other words, you are using a lie. But what it really is, it is an outgrowth of the idea that I as a businessman would say, "Grocer Johnson sells lettuce that he intentionally puts worms in because he is out to harm someone." It grows out of that idea of just injurious falsehood. It is a lie, an absolute lie. It is a harmful monstrous lie that we are dealing with here.

It is that kind of an outrage that gave rise to the drafting of this particular tort. It is injurious. It is either intentional or the legal equivalent thereof. And it is a dangerous thing that occurred here.

And the reason I see it as being different is that there is also a fallout from it. The fallout is that it benefits—it benefits the defendants in this case in this manner. And that is that by slamming this lie down upon the plaintiff, they can then—if he chooses not to respond to it, they use it. It becomes a tool in their propaganda war. And it is something different.

I believe it is viable and it is sufficiently independent to remain as a cause of action.

. . .

THE COURT: Is there anything further, Mr. Cox, that you want to stress or highlight, bearing in mind that I have read your papers and that I am going to reread a number of them? Is there anything else you want to highlight at this time on your motion for summary?

MR. COX: Well, is Your Honor inclined to take additional argument relating to the next cause of action on intentional infliction, or do you feel that that argument that we just made was—

THE COURT: I think it is pretty much one ball of wax to me. I understand the point. I think I understand the point you seek to make in differentiating.

But I think the argument is largely the same.

MR. COX: Then I believe there are some more things that I should say.

I did not truly discuss the plaintiff's point of view as it relates to—let's deal with both the injurious denial of established facts and the intentional infliction of emotional distress.

Mr. Fusilier says that since plaintiff has published one book relating to his experiences at Auschwitz, that he appears without pay and lectures at high schools and colleges, that he exercises his First Amendment rights and writes a letter for a newspaper and says who are these people; why are they doing what they are doing, that he in some way surrenders—he allows himself to be pell-melled, he allows himself to be subject to attack, some form of privilege, I suppose, some form of implied consent. This is one way of looking at this.

There is another way of looking at it. And I think it is very important to look at it in terms of the psychology, the healthiness of what Mr. Mermelstein did.

First off, we have to recognize—whether or not Your Honor grants our motion on judicial notice or not, I am not going to predicate my argument on an "as if" basis. Mr. Mermelstein went through hell. Mr. McCalden admits that. He says that Auschwitz in the summer of '44 was an incredibly horrible place. We can't detract from that. That happened.

The question is once that happened, what right have we, what privilege do we have [in] our own mind as to how we try to heal that? Because I think we have to just say that a 17-year-old boy going through that would be harmed in a grievous way.

Various people respond in different ways. But in this particular case Mr. Mermelstein responded in a healthy way. He drafted—he wrote about it; he talked about it. But he talked about it and he wrote about it in a dignified way. He talked about it and wrote about it in a way which supported him, which supported his personal primary relationship.

He in no way allowed or by doing that said you can go into anyplace in my mind and trample around in there.

We are all entitled to open up a certain recollection or a certain memory to the extent that it can be by being exposed to the fresh air perhaps in discussion and it can somehow be made better or we can close it off. But it is our option.

That is really what this case is all about; that defendants sought out and hit the person who is in the position both in tort law and criminal law as having a paper-thin skull.

Here is someone who has tried very hard to deal with this, who has done as best he could to deal with it in a psychologically healthy way. He did in fact do that.

He has built a successful small business. He has married. He has had children. He has done well in life. And then along comes this steamroller and says no, your mother and two sisters didn't die; your father and brother, they are probably all in Russia, according to Mr. McCalden, or they are alive in Israel under assumed names.

The book of Mr. Butts that they rely on so much as being authoritative applies that Jewish people—implies that what happened is marriages were breaking down. They just abandoned their spouses and children; went off and assumed other names, garbage such as that.

But this all happened. And it did happen. And I keep having to say that. I apologize to the Court. I apologize for the record that I do not have the language to explain better, to discuss it or to describe it. But it is real.

. . .

But, Your Honor, this is a matter of grave concern not only to the plaintiff, to all the people who are here today, it is a matter of concern to those thousands of survivors; it is a matter of concern from my standpoint.

As I said, there is a personal agenda here, non-Jewish agenda. And that is that it is important to the people of this country, to the people of this community, that this matter be resolved.

I don't think that Mr. Fusilier will say anything different than what I am saying here today. We want this settled. This case has gone on—I brought a part of my file here—it has gone on for over a year now. It has been discussed and has been beaten to death.

The facts are not disputed particularly. We know what happened. The only question is, is there protection within the law? It is a summary matter in a way.

We originally filed a lawsuit and attempted as best we could to calculate the damages that have been done to the plaintiffs in terms of having to go through a five-year lawsuit. We are looking at a point where we have to allege damages down the road.

Originally when the defendant corporations did not file answers to our complaint we set this matter for a default judgment. We indicated to the Court at that time that we would be certainly willing and asked for a $50,000 judgment.

At the hearing in which that came on before the Court, we said—and we stepped aside; we allowed those organizations to file answers that day and put them on notice that that was no longer the situation.

But in many respects, Your Honor, this is kind of like a small claims court of honor here today.

This is the presiding judge of the Law and Motions Department of, certainly, one of the largest courts in the country. And this is certainly going to be reported today to thousands, if not millions, of people what occurred here. That is all this case is about.

Mr. Mermelstein is not here for the money. I am not here for the money.

I think it is clear from the record that this is a *pro bono* representation on the part of my law firm.

There is a commitment on the part of both Mr. Mermelstein and I to contribute any recovery here to an appropriate charity.

This is a matter not only of honor, but it is a matter of desperation, too.

Mr. Mermelstein, you know, was one of the last victims of the Nazi Holocaust in Europe. And—

MR. FUSILIER: I object, Your Honor. That is argumentative.

THE COURT: I think this is outside the scope of argument on this particular point, Mr. Cox. I'll sustain that particular objection.

. . .

THE COURT: I am going to take the plaintiff's motion for summary adjudication under submission other than the point with respect to Mr. Brandon's status as a director.

But going back to the plaintiff's request for judicial notice—and I do not know that the ruling that I am going to make on that right now really determines conclusively any of the causes of action completely—I think the plaintiff's request is entitled to be complied with to this extent: Under Evidence Code Section 452(h) this Court does take judicial notice of the fact that Jews were gassed to death at Auschwitz Concentration Camp in Poland during the summer of 1944.

Now, that is not the entire issue in this lawsuit as I see it. And in taking that judicial notice, I am not relying on offers of proof, really, by—or declaration by—this plaintiff. It just simply is a fact that falls within the definition of Evidence Code Section 452(h).

It is not reasonably subject to dispute. And it is capable of immediate and accurate determination by resort to sources of reasonably indisputable accuracy. It is simply a fact. It does not determine this lawsuit necessarily.

MR. FUSILIER: What sources?

THE COURT: Any number of sources, any number of books, publications of really indisputable accuracy.

Otherwise, the matter stands submitted.

(D) Brief on Judicial Notice

Points and Authorities in Support of Plaintiff's Request That Court Take Judicial Notice of the Fact That Jews Were Gassed at Auschwitz

Judicial notice must be taken of facts and propositions of generalized knowledge that are so universally known that they cannot reasonably be the subject of dispute. Evid. Code Sec. 451(f).

Judicial notice may be taken of "facts and propositions that are not reasonably subject to dispute and are capable of immediate and accurate determination by resort to sources of reasonably indisputable accuracy." Evid. Code Sec. 452(h).

Where a party requests it, (a) gives each adverse party sufficient notice of the requests, through the pleading or otherwise, to enable such adverse party to prepare to meet the request, and (b) furnishes the court with sufficient information to take judicial notice of the matter, the Court shall take notice of any matter specified in Sec. 452. Evid. Code Sec. 453(a)(b).

Furthermore, under Evid. Code Sec. 454, in determining the propriety of taking judicial notice of a matter, (1) any source of pertinent information, including all advice of persons learned in the subject matter, may be consulted or used, whether or not furnished by a proxy, and (2) exclusionary rules of evidence do not apply except for Sec. 352 and the rules of privilege. Evid. Code Sec. 454(a)(1)(2).

The doctrine of judicial notice was adopted as a judicial shortcut to avoid the necessity for formal introduction of evidence in certain cases where there is not real need for such evidence. *Weitzenkorn v. Lesser*, (1953) 40 C.2d 778, 256 P.2d 947.

Judicial notice is a form of evidence. *Samaha, In re*, (1933) 130 C.A. 116, 19 P.2d 839. It extends to all proceedings in the same case, *Edwards Estate*, (1959) 173 C.A.2d 705, 344 P.2d 89, and may be relied upon to contradict other evidence and to support findings of fact on judgment based thereon, *Fawcett Estate*, (1965) 232 C.A.2d 770, 43 Cal.Rptr. 160.

Courts will take judicial notice of matter that is of common and general knowledge, but *belief need not be universal*, it being enough that matter is of common knowledge of majority of mankind, or to those persons familiar with particular matter in question. *Galloway v. Moreno*, (1960) 183 C.A.2d 804, 7 Cal.Rptr. 349. (Emphasis added)

The test is whether sufficient notoriety has attached to fact to make it proper to assume its existence without proof. *King v. Ludlow*, (1958) 165 C.A.2d 620, 332 P.2d 345.

Every judge is bound to know the history and the leading traits which enter into the history of the country where he presides. *Conger v. Weaver* (1856) 6 C 548 65 Am. Dec. 528. For example, in *People v. Mason* (1946) 72 CA 2d 699, 165 P2d 481, the court recognized the constant sabotage attempts made against American ships during World War II.

Courts commonly have taken judicial notice of historical and political facts. One such case recognized that "When Hitler came to power in 1933, he suspended the personal liberty provisions of the Weimar Constitution and . . . established an absolute dictatorship based on the tenets of national socialism." *US v. Kusche* 56 F. Supp. 201 9S.D. Cal., 1944). In *The Prohava*, 38 F. Supp. 418 (So Cal. 1941), the court took judicial notice of the occupation of Romania by Germany.

More to the point, the court in *Frankel's Estate* 92 N.Y. Supp. 2d 30 judicially noticed the commencement of brutality in the Nazi invasion of Lithuania, and that a policy of extermination of those of the Jewish faith was carried out. In a similar case, the New York court noticed "the policies of persecution and extermination practiced by the Nazis and Communists alike against individuals and groups because of their race, religion, nationality, political beliefs, or for no reason at all." *Siusin's Estate* 95 N.Y. Supp. 2d 48, 50.

Judicial notice is not only a method favored by the courts to conserve judicial energies, it is an aid to those who, like the plaintiff, is called upon to offer proof of events normally beyond the ability of individual litigants to provide. It is submitted that the murder of approximately 6,000,000 persons of Jewish religion and ethnic origin during World War II as the result of a program of genocide practiced by the National Socialistic Government as it existed in German and her captured territories before and during World War II is such an event of epic proportions. To recognize such event is required upon the presentation of property authority.

What follows in the Memorandum of Information establishes the fact that Jews were gassed to death at the Auschwitz Concentration

Camp in Poland during the summer of 1944, that such fact is a commonly known and readily verifiable fact of history, and that the court must take judicial notice thereof.

Dated: August 3, 1981

Respectfully Submitted

WILLIAM COX

Counsel for Plaintiff

MEMORANDUM OF INFORMATION REGARDING REQUEST FOR THE COURT TO TAKE JUDICIAL NOTICE (EVID. CODE SEC. 450 ET. SEQ.)

Review of Literature

"AUSCHWITZ (OW'-SHWITZ) A city in SW. Poland; site of a German extermination camp, in which, and in the nearby Birkenau camp, 1,715,000 Jews were slaughtered during World War II." *Funk & Wagnalls New Practical Standard Dictionary* Britannica World Language Editions (1955) Vol. I, Page 96.

"In Nazi Germany, concentration camps (*Konzentrationslager*) were first established for the confinement of opponents of the Nazi Party . . . But political opposition soon was enlarged to include others, particularly such persecuted minorities as the Jews. In the anti-Jewish program of 1939, 20,000 Jews were taken into 'protective custody' and sent to the concentration camps.

"The outbreak of World War II created a tremendous demand for labour in Germany, and Nazi authorities turned to the concentration camp population to augment the labour supply. From 1940 to 1942 nine new camps were established: Auschwitz . . .

"By the end of September 1944 there had been put to work in the Third Reich some 2,000,000 prisoners of war . . . and some 7,500,000 foreign civilian men, women and children . . . Although some of the non-Jewish civilians from Western Europe arrived initially as 'volunteers' . . . almost all of the millions were rounded up by force, transported to Germany in boxcars, and put to work in factories, mines, and fields under conditions that were degrading and brutal. Housing was so deplorable, rations were so meagre, and work so excessive that few persons could survive long internment." *Encyclopedia Britannica* 15th Edition, Volume 16, pp. 863,4.

In Volume III of the same Encyclopedia, further details of the concentration camps are provided.

"It is estimated that in all the camps of Nazi Germany and its occupied territories, 18,000,000 to 26,000,000 persons—prisoners of war, political prisoners, nationals of occupied and invaded countries—were put to death through hunger, cold, pestilence, torture, medical experimentation, and other means of extermination such as gas chambers

". . . The most shocking extension of this system was the establishment after 1940 of extermination centres. They were located primarily in Poland, which Hitler had selected as the scene for his final solution to the Jewish problem. The most notorious were Auschwitz, Majdanek, and Treblinka in Poland, and Buchenwald in Germany." *Encyclopaedia Britannica Volume III*, pp. 60,1.

Finally, under the heading, "Poland, History of," we find the following chilling indictment of fact:

"German policy of extermination. The extermination of the Polish intellectuals and the mass deportation of Poles, particularly from the areas around Poznan, Lodz, and Zamosc, was vigorously pursued. The Polish citizens of Jewish descent, hundreds of thousands of whom had been interned in the ghettos of the large cities, were deported to extermination camps, such as Auschwitz and Treblinka, where they were killed, along with the Jewish population of the greater part of Europe. Neither the belated ghetto risings of Warsaw, Bialystok, and Wilno (April-September 1943) nor the special actions taken by the Polish underground were effective enough to halt this extermination. According to the most careful estimates, about 3,350,000 Polish citizens of Jewish descent were slaughtered. Millions of Polish citizens were sent to forced labour camps in Germany, and hundreds of thousands were executed." *Encyclopaedia Britannica* 15th Ed., Volume 14, pp. 652,3.

Following World War II, the International Military Tribunal was convened at Nuremberg, Germany to hear the matter of war crimes committed by various Nazi leaders and organizations. These proceedings as they relate to the issue before the court are summarized in the court's findings under the heading (E) Persecution of the Jews. Taking up only five printed pages of the thousands published of the proceedings, these pages are reproduced here in their entirety because they cannot otherwise be condensed.

"The persecution of the Jews at the hands of the Nazi Government has been proved in the greatest detail before the Tribunal. It is a record of consistent and systematic inhumanity on the greatest scale. Ohlendorf, chief of Amt III in the RSHA from 1939 to 1943, and who was in command of one of the Einsatz groups in the campaign against the Soviet Union testified as to the methods employed in the extermination of the Jews. He said that he employed firing squads to shoot the victims in order to lessen the sense of individual guilt on the part of his men; and the 90,000 men, women, and children who were murdered in 1 year by his particular group were mostly Jews.

"When the witness Bach-Zelewski was asked how Ohlendorf could admit the murder of 90,000 people, he replied:

'I am of the opinion that when, for years, for decades, the doctrine is preached that the Slav race is an inferior race, and Jews not even human, then such an outcome is inevitable.'

"But the defendant Frank spoke the final words of this chapter of Nazi history when he testified in this court:

'We have fought against Jewry; we have fought against it for years; and we have allowed ourselves to make utterances and my own diary has become a witness against me in this connection—utterances which are terrible * * *. A thousand years will pass and this guilt of Germany will still not be erased.'

110

"The anti-Jewish policy was formulated in point 4 of the party program which declared, 'Only a member of the race can only be one who is of German blood, without consideration of creed. Consequently, no Jew can be a member of the race.' Other points of the program declared that Jews should be treated as foreigners, that they should not be permitted to hold public office, that they should be expelled from the Reich if it were impossible to nourish the entire population of the State, that they should be denied further immigration into Germany, and that they should be prohibited from publishing German newspapers. The Nazi Party preached these doctrines throughout its history. 'Der Stuermer' and other publications were allowed to disseminate hatred of the Jews, and in the speeches and public declarations of the Nazi leaders, the Jews were held up to public ridicule and contempt.

"With the seizure of power, the persecution of the Jews was intensified. A series of discriminatory laws was passed, which limited the offices and professions permitted to Jews; and restrictions were placed on their family life and their rights of citizenship. By the autumn of 1938, the Nazi policy towards the Jews had reached the stage where it was directed towards the complete exclusion of Jews from German life. Pogroms were organized, which included the burning and demolishing of synagogues, the looting of Jewish businesses, and the arrest of prominent Jewish businessmen. A collective fine of 1 billion marks was imposed on the Jews, the seizure of Jewish assets was authorized, and the movement of Jews was restricted by regulations to certain specified districts and hours. The creation of ghettoes was carried out on an extensive scale, and by an order of the security police Jews were compelled to wear a yellow star to be worn on the breast and back.

"It was contended for the prosecution that certain aspects of this anti-Semitic policy were connected with the plans for aggressive war. The violent measures taken against the Jews in November 1938 were nominally in retaliation for the killing of an official of the German Embassy in Paris. But the decision to seize Austria and Czechoslovakia had been made a year before. The imposition of a fine of 1 billion marks was made, and the confiscation of the financial holdings of the Jews was decreed, at a time when German armament expenditure had put the German treasury in difficulties, and when the reduction of expenditure on armaments was being considered. These steps were taken, moreover, with the approval of the defendant Goering, who had been given responsibility for economic matters of this kind, and who was the strongest advocate of an extensive rearmament program notwithstanding the financial difficulties.

"It was further said that the connection of the anti-Semitic policy with aggressive war was not limited to economic matters. The German foreign office circular, in an article of January 25, 1939, entitled 'Jewish question as a factor in German foreign policy in the year 1938,' described the new phase in the Nazi anti-Semitic policy in these words:

> 'It is certainly no coincidence that the fateful year 1938 has brought nearer the solution of the Jewish question simultaneously with the realization of the idea of Greater Germany, since the Jewish policy was both the basis and consequence of the events of the year 1938. The advance made by Jewish influence and the destructive Jewish spirit in politics, economy, and culture, paralyzed the power and the will of the German people to rise again, more perhaps even than the power policy opposition of the former enemy Allied powers of the First World War. The healing of this sickness among the people was therefore certainly one of

the most important requirements for
exerting the force which, in the year
1938, resulted in the joining together of
Greater Germany in defiance of the
world.'

"The Nazi persecution of Jews in Germany before the
war, severe and repressive as it was, cannot compare,
however, with the policy pursued during the war in the
occupied territories. Originally the policy was similar to
that which had been in force inside Germany. Jews were
required to register, were forced to live in ghettoes, to
wear the yellow star, and were used as slave laborers.
In the summer of 1941, however, plans were made for
the 'final solution' of the Jewish question in Europe.
This 'final solution' meant the extermination of the
Jews, which early in 1939 Hitler had threatened would
be one of the consequences of an outbreak of war, and a
special section of the Gestapo under Adolf Eichmann, as
head of section B-4, of the Gestapo, was formed to carry
out the policy.

"The plan for exterminating the Jews was developed
shortly after the attack on the Soviet Union.
Einsatzgruppen of the security police and SD, formed for
the purpose of breaking the resistance of the population
of the areas lying behind the German armies in the east,
were given the duty of exterminating the Jews in those
areas. The effectiveness of the work of the
Einsatzgruppen is shown by the fact that in February
1942, Heydrich was able to report that Estonia had
already been cleared of Jews and that in Riga the
number of Jews had been reduced from 29,500 to 2,500.
Altogether the *Einsatzgruppen* operating in the occupied
Baltic States killed over 135,000 Jews in 3 months.

"Nor did these special units operate completely
independently of the German armed forces. There is
clear evidence that leaders of the *Einsatzgruppen*
obtained the cooperation of army commanders. In one
case the relations between an *Einsatzgruppe* and the

military authorities was described at the time as being 'very close, almost cordial'; in another case the smoothness of an *Einsatzcommando's* operations was attributed to the 'understand for this procedure' shown by the army authorities.

"Units of the security police and SD in the occupied territories of the east, which were under civil administration, were given a similar task. The planned and systematic character of the Jewish persecutions is best illustrated by the original report of the SS Brigadier General Stroop, who was in charge of the destruction of the ghetto in Warsaw, which took place in 1943. The Tribunal received in evidence that report, illustrated with photographs, bearing on its title page: 'The Jewish Ghetto in Warsaw no longer exists.' The volume records a series of reports sent by Stroop to the higher SS and Police Fuehrer east. In April and May of 1943, in one report, Stroop wrote:

> 'The resistance put up the Jews and bandits could only be suppressed by energetic actions of our troops day and night. The Reichsfuehrer SS ordered therefore on 23 April 1943, the cleaning out of the ghetto with utter ruthlessness and merciless tenacity. I therefore decided to destroy and burn down the entire ghetto, without regard to the armament factories. These factories were systematically dismantled and then burnt. Jews usually left from their hideouts, but frequently remained in the burning buildings, and jumped out of the windows only when the heat became unbearable. They then tried to crawl with broken bones across the street into buildings which were not afire . . . Life in the sewers was not pleasant after the first week. Many times we could hear loud voices in the

sewers . . . Tear gas bombs were thrown into the manholes, and the Jews driven out of the sewers and captured. Countless numbers of Jews were liquidated in sewers and bunkers through blasting. The longer the resistance continued, the tougher became the members of the Waffen SS, Police, and Wehrmacht, who always discharged their duties in an exemplary manner.'

"Stroop recorded that his action at Warsaw eliminated 'a proven total of 56,065 people, to that we have to add the number of those killed through blasting, fire, etc., which cannot be counted.' Grim evidence of mass murders of Jews was also presented to the Tribunal in cinematograph films depicting the communal graves of hundreds of victims, which were subsequently discovered by the Allies.

"These atrocities were all part and parcel of the policy inaugurated in 1941, and it is not surprising that there should be evidence that one or two German officials entered vain protests against the brutal manner in which the killings were carried out. But the methods employed never conformed to a single pattern. The massacres of Rowno and Dubno, of which the German engineer Graebe spoke, were examples of one method; the systematic extermination of Jews in concentration camps, was another. Part of the 'final solution' was the gathering of Jews from all German occupied Europe in concentration camps. Their physical condition was the test of life or death. All who were not fit to work were destroyed in gas chambers and their bodies burnt. Certain concentration camps such as Treblinka and Auschwitz were set aside for this main purpose. With regard to Auschwitz, the Tribunal heard the evidence of Hoess, the commandant of the camp from May 1, 1940 to December 1, 1943. He estimated that in the camp of Auschwitz alone in that time 2,500,000 persons were exterminated, and that a further 500,000 died from disease and starvation. Hoess described the screening for extermination by stating in evidence:

'We had two SS doctors on duty at Auschwitz to examine incoming transports of prisoners. The prisoners would be marched by one of the doctors who would make spot decisions as they walked by. Those who were fit for work were sent into the camp. Others were sent immediately to the extermination plants. Children of tender years were invariably exterminated since by reason of their youth there were unable to work. Still another improvement we made over Treblinka was that at Treblinka the victims almost always knew they were to be exterminated and at Auschwitz we endeavored to fool the victims into thinking that they were to go through a delousing process. Of course, frequently they realized our true intentions and we sometimes had riots and difficulties due to that fact. Very frequently women would hide their children under their clothes, but of course when we found them we would send the children in to be exterminated.'" NAZI CONSPIRACY AND AGGRESSION, Opinion and Judgment Office of United States Chief of Counsel for Prosecution of Axis Criminality (1947) Pages 77-81.

The trials of Nazi war criminals did not end in 1947. They have continued until this day. On December 20, 1963, twenty-two former SS men were tried in the criminal court of Frankfurt, West Germany for their roles in the "final solution to the Jewish problem." There, as in all of the trials held on the subject, the fact of extermination was not denied, only the individual defendants' complicity was in issue. The "Auschwitz Trial," as it became known, lasted for twenty months. There were twenty convictions and two acquittals. In determining its jurisdiction, the court stated, as follows, in its opinion:

> ". . . The German Federal Republic because of this continuity of identity is the successor of the German Reich. This state has been in existence from 1871 to the Weimar Republic to the Federal Republic and has always had the same penal code. Under this penal code murder has always been a punishable offense. National Socialism did exercise all-embracing power in Germany, but this did not give it the right to turn wrong into right. In particular, it could not determine that a deed bearing all the earmarks of a punishable offense was not an injustice because it had been ordered by a specific person—even though that person may have been the sole ruler of the country. National Socialism was also subject to the rule of law. This holds true in particular on the question of the 'final solution of the Jewish problem.'" *Auschwitz*: A Report on the Proceedings Against Robert Karl Ludwig Mulka and Others before the Court of Frankfurt, Bernd Naumann, p. 415.

In its opinion, the court reviewed the incredible difficulty of having to rely almost exclusively upon eyewitness accounts; however the awesomeness of the crimes can be seen by a look at the findings as to just one defendant, Robert Mulka, who served as an adjutant at Auschwitz in 1942.

> "'It could not be established whether defendant Mulka had himself conducted a selection. But that he did have a part in the procurement of Zyklon B is clearly established by Order No. 13, dated October 2, 1942.' There can also be no doubt that he was in charge of the motor pool, 'that he knew the job the motor pool was doing, particularly that he made available the trucks for the transport of new arrivals to the gas chambers. Also, the defendant received and passed on teletypes announcing the arrival of transports; and he worked on the construction of the crematories.' He was aware of

the illegal nature of these murders; according to his own
testimony he called them a blatant injustice and crime.
By his own admission he had selected on the ramp at
least three times and thus helped set in motion the
subsequent events. 'The court has estimated the size of
these transports at 1,000, and worked on the assumption
that at least one quarter—i.e., 250—were selected for the
labor camp, so that in each case 750 persons faced
extermination, and that the defendant was an accessory
to that.'" *Auschwitz:* A Report on the Proceedings
Against Robert Karl Ludwig Mulka and Others before
the Court of Frankfurt, Bernd Naumann, p. 418.

Perhaps the most famous postwar trial took place in Jerusalem in
1960, when Adolf Eichmann was brought to trial for his role as the Chief
of the Jewish Affairs Bureau of the SS, the executive arm for the Final
Solution. While the declaration of Gideon Hausner, the prosecutor, is
attached, the following excerpts from his book establish the level of
inquiry that went into establishing the extent of the Holocaust.

"Poison gas had already been in use in Germany for
some time. The Nazis had a scheme for killing the
mentally insane which they called mercy killing or
euthanasia; apparently they could hardly wait for the
smoke screen of war to put it into effect. By an order
dated September 1, 1939—the very day war broke
out—Hitler authorized the Chief of his Chancellery,
Buehler, and his private physician, Dr. Brandt, to
administer 'mercy killing' to incurable persons. The
order was implemented by Brack, of Hitler's
Chancellery, who employed for the purpose an officer
of the Stuttgart police, Kriminalkommissar Wirth. It was
Wirth's job to carry out the killing by using carbon
monoxide gas. He was later transferred to the Lublin
camps and placed under the orders of Globocnik.

Others, too, were seeking a 'cleaner' way to dispose of
the Jews. Among them was Dr. Erhard Wetzel, a senior
official of the Ministry for the Eastern Territories. He
reported on October 25, 1941, that after consultations
with Brack and Eichmann the three of them had decided

to use poison gas for killing Jews. Brack had promised to assist by putting up the installations and by sending his expert, Dr. Kellmeyer, to Riga. It was decided, Wetzel added, to use 'the Black method' on the 'unfit' Jews in the East. It was only awhile later that Wetzel's superior, the Commissioner for the East, forbade all officials of his Ministry to take any part in the execution of the Jews, 'this being the exclusive duty of the Security Police.'

"Hoess, the Commandant of Auschwitz, was engaged in experiments of his own in search of a method of quick mass killings. In the summer of 1941, he was summoned by Himmler, who told him that the Fuehrer had ordered the killing of the Jews and that the SS would carry out the order. In Himmler's opinion, the existing extermination methods in the East were inadequate for this large-scale operation, and Auschwitz had therefore been earmarked for the purpose, because of its geographical location and the ease with which could be camouflaged. Hoess was also told that he had been personally entrusted with the task, which called for supreme devotion. Himmler added a significant statement: 'You will learn further details from SS Lieutenant Colonel Eichmann of the RSHA, who will call on you in the immediate future.'

"Hoess recalled in his autobiography that shortly afterward Eichmann came to see him in Auschwitz and disclosed the plans for the operation, which had to cover deportees from numerous countries. They discussed possible ways and means, and agreed that all the killing would be done by gassing. 'Eichmann told me about the method of killing people with exhaust gases in trucks, which had been previously used in the East,' Hoess wrote. But this was inadequate for the masses of people who were due to arrive in Auschwitz. 'The use of carbon monoxide, as was done with mental patients in some places in the Reich, will necessitate too many buildings,' he added; so this method too was discarded. The matter was left unresolved, and

Eichmann decided to try to find a gas that was readily available and would not require special installation for its use.

"At the end of November, 1941, Hoess continued, he was summoned to a conference in Berlin attended by all of Eichmann's assistants. It appeared that Eichmann had not yet discovered a suitable kind of gas. But while Hoess was away, his assistant tried out 'Cyclon B' gas on Russian prisoners of war; he found it dispatched victims instantly. Eichmann was immediately notified and rushed to Auschwitz. After a thorough discussion and inspection on the spot, the two men decided to employ this method for the mass extermination.

"At a later stage a dispute developed on the respective merits of the 'Cyclon B' and 'exhaust gas' systems. Wirth regarded Hoess as his 'untalented pupil', while Hoess was able to point to the greater speed and certainty of his method. Eichmann's department preferred the 'Cyclon B' and contacted an expert to assist them in getting it and introducing it throughout the camps. His name was Kurt Gerstein. He was an engineer who had some trouble with the Gestapo in the prewar years. He had spoken out somewhat freely about some of the Nazi measures and been interrogated and even detained for awhile as a result. When one of his relatives died suddenly in a lunatic asylum, he decided to find out for himself the truth about the alleged exterminations. So he volunteered to join the sanitation department of the SS. Soon after he had taken up his post, Rolf Guenther, Eichmann's deputy, called on him and asked for 100 kilograms of poison gas to be supplied immediately to Eichmann's headquarters at Kurfueratenstrasse 116. 'Nobody should know about it and you will have to accompany the transport personally' were Guenther's instructions.

"He further requested Gertstein to proceed immediately to the Belzec camp to carry out an inspection and to make the necessary arrangements for improving the methods of killing they were using there." *Justice in Jerusalem*, pp. 90-91.

Specifically in relation to Auschwitz, Hausner's investigation revealed:

"Auschwitz-Birkenau was the peak of all horror. Initially designated as the place of destruction of European Jewry, it soon spread out over a 'sphere of interests' (*Interessengebiet*) that covered over fifteen square miles of territory between the rivers Vistula and Sola. Eight villages and a town were evacuated to accommodate a colossal industrial complex, comprising Krupp's Union armament plants, I.G. Farbenindustrie's Buna synthetic petrol and rubber works, chemical and metal factories, gas works and railway repair shops, besides quarries and hydraulic, agricultural and timber enterprises. It serviced, apart from the 'mother encampment,' thirty-nine ramifications, scattered all over Silesia.

"But its main output was death. Three and a half million people were liquidated there in the three years of its activity.

"On arrival at Auschwitz, a prisoner would have a number tattooed on his arm if he was to be left alive for awhile to work. His number became the name under which he would henceforth be known. The uniformed Germans were his omnipotent gods. The Kapos and 'Blockaelteste,' whom the SS appointed from among the prisoners were powerful authorities. An inmate was a speck of dust, which existed only so long as one of these superior beings did not care to brush it off. His total insignificance was made clear from the moment of his arrival. 'Here you are allowed to do only what you are told to do. Whatever you are not ordered to do is strictly forbidden and severely punishable,' they were told. They would be drilled for hours on end to take their caps off before every SS man, whom they were allowed to pass only in military tempo, bareheaded, and not closer than six paces with arms stiff and held tightly to the body.

"Then they made the immediate acquaintance of the punishment system, and were given a garment, which soon became stinking and vermin-covered, and wooden clogs. The cap was all-important; it served both for saluting and for dishing out food, and its color, in addition to other signs, disclosed the prisoner's standing in the hierarchy. So did the whip carried by everyone in authority. It was soon apparent to the new arrival that in order to be 'somebody' on this planet it was necessary to be sadistically cruel. Thus a man could rise to be a '*Stubenaelteste*,' responsible for a room, and get an extra dish of soup. He could go further and become the '*Blockschreiber*,' the clerk responsible for counting the prisoners, or even the '*Blockaelteste*,' responsible for the whole block. A '*Lageraelteste*' was the head prisoner. At work some prisoners were 'Kapos', the labor foreman, who had complete power of life and death over every inmate. These were often recruited from among the habitual criminals.

"But these rules concerned only those who had passed the first selection screening at the railway siding on arrival and were considered fit for work. All others were sent straight to one of the four crematoria, which together comprised forty-six ovens and could handle over five hundred bodies per hour. These people were not accounted for in the camp's registration office. Only a prisoner who was to live for awhile and got his tattooed number was 'recognized' in the record of his arrivals. When he was later sent to be gassed, his card would be removed and stamped with the letters 'S.B'—'*Sonderbehandlung*' ('Special Treatment'). If he was shot, hanged or whipped to death, or if he died of hunger, the record stated that he had succumbed to pneumonia, heart failure or dysentery. According to the register no one in the camp had ever come to an unnatural end there.

"But even these records once led to embarrassment because of bureaucratic efficiency. The Bureaus of Vital Statistics in Germany used to exchange data. One day a letter came from the Oldenburg bureau suggesting that there must be some mistake in the data of the Auschwitz bureau, which showed so many deaths for such a small place. Ten days later the Thueringen bureau wrote that the Auschwitz registration office in its inexperience must have ascribed to one year all the deaths that had occurred there since 1870, when the bureaus were first established in Germany, as otherwise the large numbers were inexplicable. This, it was pointed out, was not the correct procedure. The Auschwitz office chief was alarmed, but he found a solution for the problem. He simply adopted a code for registrations by every 180 deaths were recorded as one in the statistical forms that were sent out." *Justice in Jerusalem*, pp. 169-171.

Perhaps the most commonly read modern biography of Adolf Hitler is the book by the same title published by John Toland in 1976. There, beginning on page 958, he gives us insight into how the horrible murder machine we came to call the Holocaust began:

"Two days after the invasion of the Soviet Union the man responsible for the deportation of Jews, Reinhard Heydrich, complained in writing that this was no answer to the Jewish problem. Deporting these misfits to the French island of Madagascar, for instance, would have to be dropped in favor of a more practical solution. It was fitting, therefore, that on the last day of July Heydrich received a cryptic order (signed by Goring upon instructions from the Fuhrer) instructing him 'to make all necessary preparations regarding organizations and financial matters to bring about a complete solution of the Jewish question in the German sphere of influence in Europe.' (Footnote omitted.)

"Behind the innocuous bureaucratic language lay sweeping authority for the SS to organize the extermination of European Jewry. As a preliminary step, Himmler—still shaken by his experience in

Minsk—asked the chief physician of the SS what was the best method of mass extermination. The answer was: gas chambers. The next step was to summon Rudolf Hoss [Hoess or Hess], the commandant of the largest concentration camp in Poland, and give him secret oral instructions. 'He told me,' testified Hoss, 'something to the effect—I do not remember the exact words—that the Fuehrer had given the order for a final solution of the Jewish question. We, the SS, must carry out that order. If it is not carried out now the Jews will later on destroy the German people.' Himmler said he had chosen Hoss's camp since Auschwitz, strategically located near the border of German, afforded space for measures requiring isolation. Hoss warned that this operation was to be treated as a secret Reich matter. He was forbidden to discuss the matter with his immediate superior. And so Hoss returned to Poland and, behind the back of the inspector of concentration camps, quietly began to expand his grounds with intent to turn them into the greatest killing center in man's history. He did not even tell his wife what he was doing.

Hitler's concept of concentration camps as well as the practicality of genocide owed much, so he claimed, to his studies of English and United States history. He admired the camps for Boer prisoners in South Africa and for the Indians in the wild West; and often praised to his inner circle the efficiency of America's extermination—by starvation and uneven combat—of the red savages who could not be tamed by captivity.

"Until now he had scrupulously integrated his own general policy with that of Germany, since both led in the same general direction. The resurgence of German honor and military might, the seizure of lost Germanic territories, and even *Legenstrum* in the East were approved heartily by most of his countrymen. But at last had come the crossroads where Hitler must take his personal detour and solve, once and for all, the Jewish Question. While many Germans were willing to join this racist crusade, the great majority merely wanted a continuation of the limited Jewish persecution which had already received the tacit approval of millions of Westerners.

"It was Hitler's intent to start eliminating the Jews secretly before leaking out the truth a little at a time to his own people. Eventually the time would be ripe for revelations that would tie all Germans to his own fate; his destiny would become Germany's. Complicity in his crusade to cleanse Europe of Jewry would make it a national mission and rouse the people to greater efforts and sacrifices. It would also burn all bridges behind the hesitant and weak-hearted.

"Until now all this was kept secret from Hitler's innermost circle—the secretaries, adjutants, servants and personal staff. But in the autumn of 1941, the Fuehrer began making overt remarks during his table conversations, perhaps as an experiment in revelation. In mid-October, after lecturing on the necessity of bring decency into civil life, he said, 'But the first thing, above all, is to get rid of the Jews. Without that, it will be useless to clean the Augean stables.' Two days later he was more explicit. 'From the rostrum of the Reichstag, I prophesied to Jewry that, in the event of war's proving inevitable, the Jew would disappear from Europe. That race of criminals has on its conscience the two million dead of the First World War, and now already hundreds and thousands more. Let nobody tell me that all the same we can't park them in the marshy parts of Russia: Who's worrying about our troops? It's not a bad idea, by the way, that public rumor attributes to us a plan to exterminate the Jews. Terror is a salutary thing.' He predicted that the attempt to create a Jewish state would be a failure. 'I have numerous accounts to settle, about which I cannot think today. But that doesn't mean I forget them. I write them down. The time will come to bring out the big book. Even with regard to the Jews, I've found myself remaining inactive. There's no sense in adding uselessly to the difficulties of the moment. One acts shrewdly when one bides one's time.'

"One reason Hitler had delayed implementing the Final Solution was hope that his implied threat to exterminate the Jews would keep Roosevelt out of the war. But Pearl Harbor ended this faint expectation and Hitler's hope turned into bitterness, with extermination becoming a form of international reprisal.

The decision taken, the Fuehrer made it known that those entrusted with the Final Solution that the killings should be done as humanely as possible. This was in line with his conviction that he was observing God's injunction to cleanse the world of vermin. Still a member in good standing of the Church of Rome despite detestation of its hierarchy ('I am now as before a Catholic and will always remain so') he carried within him its teaching that the Jew was the killer of God. The extermination, therefore, could be done without a twinge of conscience since he was merely acting as the avenging hand of God—so long as it was done impersonally, without cruelty. Himmler was pleased to devise gas chambers which would eliminate masses of Jews efficiently and 'humanely,' then crowded the victims into boxcars and sent them east to stay in ghettos until the killing centers in Poland were completed.

"The time had come to establish the bureaucracy of liquidation and the man in charge, Heydrich, sent out invitations to a number of state secretaries and chiefs of the SS main offices for a 'Final Solution' Conference to take place on December 10, 1941. The recipients of his invitation, aware only that Jews were being deported to the East, had little idea of the meaning of 'final solution' and awaited the conference with expectation and keen interest.

"Their curiosity was whetted by a six-week postponement. Frank, head of the

Generalgouvernement (German-occupied Poland), became so impatient that he sent Philipp Bouhler, his deputy, to Heydrich for more details, then convened a conference of his own at Cracow in mid-December. 'I want to say to you quite openly,' said Hitler's former lawyer, 'that we shall have to finish the Jews, one way or another.' He told about the important conference soon to take place in Berlin which Bouhler would attend for the Generalgouvernement. 'Certainly the major migration is about to start. But what is to happen to the Jews? Do you think they will actually be settled in Eastern villages? We were told in Berlin, 'Why all this fuss? We can't use them in the Ostland either; let the dead bury their dead!' He urged his listeners to arm themselves against all feelings of sympathy. 'We have to annihilate the Jews wherever we find them and wherever it is at all possible.' It was a gigantic task and could not be carried out by legal methods. Judges and courts could not take the heavy responsibility for such an extreme policy. He estimated—and it was a gross overestimate—that there were 3,500,000 Jews in the Generalgouvernement alone. 'We can't shoot these 3,500,000 Jews, we can't poison them, but we can take steps which, one way or another, will lead to an annihilation success, and I am referring to the measures under discussion in the Reich. The Generalgouvernement will have to become just as free of Jews as the Reich itself. Where and how this is going to happen is the task for the agencies which we will have to create and establish here, and I am going to tell you how they will work when the time comes.'

"When Bouhler arrived in Berlin on January 20, 1942, for the Heydrich conference he was far better prepared than most of the conferees to understand the generalities uttered. At about 11 A.M. fifteen men gathered in a room at the Reich Security Main Office at number 56-58 Grossen Wannsee. There were representatives from Rosenberg's East Ministry, Goring's Four-Year Plan agency, the Interior Ministry, the Justice Ministry, the Foreign Office and the party chancellery. Once they had seated themselves informally at tables, Chairman Heydrich began to speak. He had been given, he said, 'the responsibility for working out the Final Solution of the Jewish problem regardless of geographical boundaries.' This euphemism was followed by a veiled and puzzling remark which involved Hitler himself. 'Instead of emigration,' he said, 'there is now a further possible solution to which the Fuhrer has already signified his consent—namely deportation to the East.'

"At this point Heydrich exhibited a chart indicating which Jewish communities were to be evacuated, and gave a hint of their fate. Those fit to work would be formed into labor gangs but even those who survived the rigors would not be allowed to go free and so 'form a new germ cell from which the Jewish race would again arise. History teaches us that.' George Leibbrandt, of Rosenberg's office, was at a loss. Martin Luther of the Foreign Office was also confused. He protested that mass Jewish evacuations would create grave difficulties in such countries as Denmark and Norway. Why not confine the deportation to the Balkans and western Europe? The conferees left Berlin with a variety of impressions. Bouhler knew exactly what Heydrich was talking about but Luther assured Fritz Hesse that there were no plans at all to kill the Jews. Leibbrandt and his superior, Alfred Meyer, gave a similar report to Rosenberg. Not a word, they agreed, had been said of extermination.

"Thirty copies of the conference record were distributed to the ministries and SS main offices and the term 'Final Solution' became known throughout the Reich bureaucracy; yet the true meaning of what Heydrich had said was fathomed only by those privy to the killing operations, and many of this select group, curiously, were convinced that Adolf Hitler himself was not totally aware that mass murder was being plotted. SS

Lieutenant Colonel Adolf Eichmann, in charge of the Gestapo's Jewish Evacuation Office, for one knew this was a myth. After the Wannsee conference he sat 'cozily around a fireplace' with Gestapo Chief Muller and Heydrich, drinking and singing songs. 'After a while we climbed onto the chairs and drank a toast; then onto the table and traipsed round and round—on the chairs and on the table again.' Eichmann joined in this celebration with no qualms. 'At that moment,' he later testified, 'I sensed a kind of Pontius Pilate feeling, for I was free of all guilt . . . Who was I to judge? Who was I to have my own thoughts in this matter?' He, Muller and Heydrich were only carrying out he laws of the land as prescribed by the Fuehrer himself.

"A few days later Hitler confirmed in spite of himself, that he was indeed the architect of the Final Solution. 'One must act radically,' he said at lunch on January 23, in the presence of Himmler. 'When one pulls out a tooth, one does it with a single tug, and the pain quickly goes away. The Jew must clear out of Europe. It's the Jew who prevents everything. When I think about it, I realize that I'm extraordinarily humane. At the time of the rules of the Popes the Jews were mistreated in Rome. Until 1830, eight Jews mounted on donkeys were led once a year through the streets of Rome. For my part, I restrict myself to telling them they must go away. If they break their pipes on the journey, I can't do anything about it. But if they refuse to go voluntarily I see no other solution but extermination.' Never before had he talked so openly to his inner circle and he was so absorbed by the subject that on the twenty-seventh he again demanded the disappearance of all Jews from Europe.

"His obsession with Jews was publicly expressed a few days later in a speech at the Sportpalast on the ninth anniversary of National Socialism's rise to power. 'I do not even want to speak of the Jews,' he said, and proceeded to do so at length. 'They are simply our old enemies, their plans have suffered shipwreck though us, and they rightly hate us, just as we hate them. We realize that this war can only end either in the wiping out of the Germanic nations, or by the disappearance of Jewry from Europe.' He reminded the audience, which included some forty high-ranking military officers, of his 1939 prophecy that the Jews would be destroyed. 'For the first time, it will not be the others who will bleed to death, but for the first time the genuine ancient Jewish law, 'an eye for an eye, a tooth for a tooth,' is being applied. The more this struggle spreads, the more anti-Semitism will spread—and world Jewry may rely on this. It will find nourishment in every prison camp, it will find nourishment in every family which is being enlightened as to why it is being called upon to make such sacrifices, and the hour will come when the worst enemy in the world will have finished his part for at least a thousand years to come.'

"To those presently engaged in designing gas chambers, to those constructing the killing centers in Poland, and particularly to those who were being prepared to administer the mechanics of the final solution, this statement was a clarion call for genocide. But to foreign observers, such as Arvid Fredborg, Hitler's words and appearance that afternoon seemed to foreshadow a German disaster. 'His face,' wrote the Swedish journalist, 'now seemed ravaged and his manner uncertain.'" *Adolf Hitler*, pp. 958-965.

Finally, the court is directed to the following books from which pages have been copied and attached to this memorandum:

1. *We Have Not Forgotten* (Polonia Publishing House), Warsaw, 1962. Page 108 (bottom left) Photograph: "Women on the way to the gas chamber. This photograph was taken secretly by the prisoner David Szmulewski, a member of the resistance movement." (Oswiecim/Auschwitz).

2. *La Deportation*—Edition le Patriote Resistant Federational Nationale des Deportes at Internen Resistants et Patriotes (FNDIRP) Paris, 1978. Page 212 (bottom) Photograph: Caption: "Ces hommes, ces femmes, ces enfants diriges vers les chambres a gaz d'Auschwitz attendant ici le moment du deshabillage. Leur Crume: etre juifs. (Photo prise en 1944, par un S.S.; son album retrouve figure aux archives du Musee d'Auschwitz. Translation: These men, these women, these children directed toward the gas chambers of Auschwitz here await undressing. Their crime: to be Jews. (Photo taken by an S.S. man; his album is part of the Archives of the Museum of Auschwitz).

3. *Auschwitz 1940-1945*, Guidebook through the Museum Kazimierz Smolen, State Museum in Oswiecim (Auschwitz Birkenau.) Pages 25-35: Description of the process of Selection and Extermination. Page 105: Description of gassing of Jews from Terezin, March 9, July 11 and 12, 1944.

4. *The Investigation of Nazi Crimes 1945-1978,* C. F. Muller. A Documentation.

5. *KL Auschwitz Seen by the S.S.,* Hoess, Rudolph; Broad, Kremer; Czech, D. and Bezwinska, J., Publication of Panstwowe Muzeum in Oswiecim - (1978). Pages 133-136: Description by Rudolf Hoess, Commandant of Auschwitz of the extermination process.

6. *The Holocaust and the New-Nazi Mythomania,* Klarsfeld, Serge, ed. (1978, Paris) Pages 109-119: "The Existence of Gas Chambers."

7. *The Crime and Punishment of I.G. Farben,* Joseph Borkin, Chapter 61 "Slave Labor and Mass Murder."

8. *Auschwitz-Birkenau Concentration Camp,* Jan Sehn (Warsaw 1961), Chapter IX "Selections" Pages 88-93.

9. *Auschwitz: Nazi Extermination Camp* (Interpress Publishers, Warsaw, 1978) Pages 111-127: "The Gas Chambers and Crematoria."

10. *KZ Auschwitz: Reminiscences of an S.S. Man* Pery Broad (Panstowe Muzeum Oswiecim, 1965) Pages 69-73 "The Death Factory".

11. *Le Memorial de la Deportation des Juifa de France* S. Klarsfield (Paris 1978) Chronological listing of transports of French Jews deported to Auschwitz, 1942-1944, including the number gassed upon arrival; Transport # 66-77 departed to Auschwitz in 1944.

DECLARATIONS OF INDIVIDUALS

Counsel for plaintiff has undertaken to include with this memorandum of information, signed declarations by various individuals, survivors, and historians to provide a cross section of opinions to aid the court in its recognition of established historical fact. These declarations are attached and include the following: (See Attachment Nos. 12 through 19.)

1. SIMON WIESENTHAL—"There was not one trial in Germany and in Austria where doubts appeared about the existence of gas chambers for the only purpose to murder people. Not even one defendant denied the existence of gas chambers, neither during the Auschwitz trial in Frankfurt, nor during the Treblinka trial in Düsseldorf, nor during the Auschwitz trial in Vienna, nor during the several Mauthausen trials. The defendants only challenged that they were involved in killing people. There was not one lawyer who tried in his defense to deny the existence of gas chambers during these trials."

2. GIDEON HAUSNER—"In view of the numerous pronouncements on the subject and in view of the vast body of credible literature and history books dealing with the subject, the fact that the Holocaust did take place, ought by now be judicially noted as an established historical fact."

3. DR. JOHN K. ROTH—"I have studied carefully the arguments made by the Institute of Historical Review, A. R. Butz, and others who dispute the fact of the gassings and the genocide. My findings are that their claims are from start to finish based on inaccurate data, calculated misinterpretations of sound existing scholarship, invalid arguments, and specious assumptions. Anyone who looks at the evidence objectively will be led inexorably to the conclusion that gassing Jews to death was the chief means the Nazis employed to achieve what they called the "Final Solution," and that final solution was to a great extent

attempted by gassing Jews at Auschwitz in the period from 1943-1945."

4. DR. GEORGE M. KREN—"The problems which occupy historians and other scholars dealing with the Holocaust have nothing to do with establishing that it happened. Nor are there many outstanding 'factual' issues which require resolution. Rather the main emphasis of Holocaust studies has been with motives, with comprehending the psychology of those involved, both victims and perpetrators, and with the larger issue of placing these events in a broader historical perspective. Thus while the reality of Hitler's anti-Semitism and commitment to a racially based eugenic policy is beyond dispute, the personal psychological, the political and social source of these views still require elaboration and analysis. The participation of many individuals in the mass killings with apparently few difficulties is beyond question; the psychological foundations of these actions—whether simple obedience, peer pressure, ideological commitment or sadism—are still in need of study. On a broader level the Holocaust has called into question the concept of progress, the view that historical development also means a moral advance towards more humane and 'civilized' modes of existence. At the same time the previously held view that human nature was essentially good and nondestructive and that destructive behavior could be explained by flaws in the social and political infrastructure has been challenged by the events of the Holocaust in favor of such more negative view of the essence of human nature."

5. PROFESSOR DR. MARTIN BROSZAT—"I have studied anti-Jewish Nazi policy for more than twenty-five years and have also read a good deal of the apologetic literature which was written by more or less extremist authors on this topic in Germany and abroad in recent years. (Ressinier, Butz, Staaglich, et al.), attempting to deny the fact of the Holocaust and especially the gassing of Jews in certain annihilation

camps (Auschwitz, Treblinka, Belzec, Sobibor, Majdanek, Chelmno). Weighing the authentic sources and this literature I come to the conclusion that there is an overwhelming evidence for the historical fact of the killing of millions of Jews by execution-squads, by gassing or by other means, mostly on the commands of the SS- and the Security-Police in the years 1941 until 1944. These established historical facts can, that is my scholarly founded opinion, by no means be annulled by artificial but none the less systematically spread doubts and critics which generally miss either a solid historical source-basis or a scholarly way of using and interpreting them, or both."

6. DR. YSRAEL GUTMAN—"The problem for the serious historian has not been the search for documentation of the fact of the genocide committed by the Nazis against Jews and others. The documentation is unlimited. The problem, the area of study for the serious historian, is in determining how the German Nazi party came to the decision to implement the so-called "final solution," in determining who was responsible for that decision, and the reasons for it. The serious historian is interested in the motivations, the psychological structure of the people who performed these acts, and in the problems and changes experienced by the person living in the concentration camp. The serious historian wishes to study how the Jews were captured and sent to the camps, and who had and did not have knowledge of what was going on. In other words, the question for the historian is a problem of cause, of method, of effect. The question of the gassing is not a question at all; it is the universally accepted historical fact from which all legitimate questions arise."

7. MAURICE GOLDSTEIN—"I was arrested by the Gestapo at my home in Brussels in September 1943 and taken together with my wife, Helen, nee Fidler to Dossin Barracks at Malines (Belgium). I there found my parents and my elder brother who had also been arrested the same day.

THE HOLOCAUST CASE: DEFEAT OF DENIAL

We all left Dossin Barracks on 20 September 1943 and were transported together in sealed cattle trucks which were hermetically closed to a then unknown destination. The train transported 1,425 people, among whom there were men, women and children, the old, sick and invalid. We arrived at our destination three days later, which was Auschwitz-Birkenau.

We were brutally told to leave our cattle trucks. On the arrival platform in the camp, an SS doctor put us through a process of selection, dividing the 1425 new arrivals into two groups. 548 men and women were considered to be fit for work and entered the camp of Birkenau on foot (Auschwitz II); there they were tattooed with their serial numbers as follows: the men from 151 481 to 151 851 & women from 62 805 to 62 983.

The 877 other arrivals, including children, pregnant women, the old and the sick, did not enter the camp but were taken away by truck; there were never registered in the records of Auschwitz, were not given tattooed serial numbers and were never seen again. This group included my mother and my pregnant wife; 51 of those who had been deported or 3.5% out of 1,425 people, got back to Belgium."

8. ROSA EHRLICH—"Everyone at Auschwitz camps I and II knew that live human beings arriving from all over Europe were being gassed day and night together—those who had been selected for gassing among the inmates of the camp. This was no secret for anyone and no one had the slightest doubt about it. Everyone, from the highest SS officer down to the lowest ranking SS employee, not to speak of all the inmates who had been deported to Auschwitz, knew that human beings were being gassed alive there; there was not a person in the camp who did not know exactly what being selected for the gas chambers meant. "

ANALYSIS OF DEFENDANT'S LITERATURE

Defendant Institute for Historical Review has published a series of professional journals on the subject of the Holocaust. During discovery, it was admitted that the journal articles reflected the best thinking and evidence on the assertion that it [the Holocaust] is but a myth. In an attempt to analyze what is presented in those journals as it relates to the subject of this motion, counsel for plaintiff engaged an expert in the English language to read and comment upon the contents. The declaration of MARY BRENNAN was heretofore submitted to the court at the previously scheduled default hearing on June 3, 1981; however, it is hereby incorporated by reference as though fully set forth and attached.

In her general conclusions, Dr. Brennan discusses the defendant's literature as follows:

> "The writers represented here are, almost without exception, ill-fitted for the task of presenting complex problem in constructive and coherent essays. Many of them, like Butz, are dealing in matters outside their acknowledged field of expertise. They would be considered unfitted for inclusion in any highly-respected Historical Journal of repute. In the present case, they seem to feed upon each other's neuroses; from Kremer to Butz, they are characterized by an overwhelming pre-occupation with minutiae. In the case of Kremer, it was stump-tailed cats. With Butz *et alia* it is using suspect information obtained from questionable sources as a foundation for yet another, one-sided attack on Zionism and its proponents.

> "Ultimately, *The Journal* is a highly propagandistic organ used for voicing the views of a handful of propagandists. It is equally as damaging as much of the anti-Semitic literature disseminated by the Nazi Regime of Germany before and during World War II used to promulgate racial and ethnic hatred.

> "As such, *The Journal,* coated in its innocent-seeming cover of artificial slickness, appeals to minds already made up; it reaches those who seek in its pages corroboration, not enlightenment; and, fosters in those

whose outlets for creative thinking are plugged up by prejudice, narrow-mindedness, and the bases of all emotions: hatred, fear, and violence." Pages 23-24 (See Att. No. 20.)

OTHER SIGNIFICANT INFORMATION

On February 24, 1979, the *Los Angeles Times* published two aerial photographs taken by the American Air Force between April 1944 and January 1945. The accompanying story explains the efforts of two analysts of the Central Intelligence Agency to use modern interpretation methods to identify not only the gas chambers, but the groups of prisoners being herded into them as well. A copy of the article is attached. (See Att. No. 21.)

On September 27, 1979, the President's Commission on the Holocaust issued its report to the President. Its findings on "The Uniqueness of the Holocaust" are repeated here in part:

> "The Holocaust was the systematic, bureaucratic extermination of six million Jews by the Nazis and their collaborators as a central act of state during the Second World War; as night descended, millions of other peoples were swept into its net of death. It was a crime unique in the annals of human history, different not only in the quantity of violence—the sheer numbers killed—but in its manner and purpose as a mass criminal enterprise organized by the state against defenseless civilian populations. The decision was to kill every Jew everywhere in Europe: the definition of Jew as targets for death transcended all boundaries. There is evidence indicating that the Nazis intended ultimately to wipe out the Slavs and other peoples; had the war continued or had the Nazis triumphed, Jews might not have remained the final victims of Nazi genocide, but they were certainly its first.

> "The concept of the annihilation of an entire people, as distinguished from their subjugation, was unprecedented; never before in human history had genocide been an all-pervasive government policy

unaffected by territorial or economic advantage and unchecked by moral or religious constraints. Ordinarily, acts of violence directed by a government against a populace are related to perceived needs of national security or geographic expansion, with hostilities diminishing after the enemy surrenders. In the case of the Nazis, however, violence was intensified after subjugation, especially in Poland and other parts of Eastern Europe, against all the subjugated populations. Jews were particular targets despite the fact that they possessed no army and were not an integral part of the military struggle. Indeed, the destruction frequently conflicted with and took priority over the war effort. Trains that could have been used to carry munitions to the front or to retrieve injured soldiers were diverted for the transport of victims to the death camps. Even after the Nazi defeat on the Russian front, when it became evident that the Germans had lost the war, the killings were intensified in a last desperate attempt at complete annihilation. Clearly, genocide was an end in itself independent of the requisites of war.

"In the Nazi program of genocide, Jews were the primary victims, exterminated not for what they were but for the fact that they were Jews. (In the Nuremberg Decree of 1935, a Jew was defined by his grandparents' affiliation. Even conversion to Christianity did not affect the Nazi definition.) While Gypsies were killed throughout Europe, Nazi plans for their extermination were never completed nor fully implemented. However, Nazi plans for the annihilation of European Jews were not only completed but thoroughly implemented. Many Polish children whose parents were killed were subjected to forced Germanization—that is, adoption by German families and assimilation into German culture—yet Jewish children were offered no such alternative to death.

"The Holocaust was not a throwback to medieval torture or archaic barbarism but a thoroughly modern expression of bureaucratic organization, industrial management, scientific achievement, and technological sophistication. The entire apparatus of the German bureaucracy was marshaled in the service of the extermination process. The churches and health ministries supplied birth records to define and isolate Jews; the post delivered statements of definition, expropriation, denaturalization, and deportation; the economic ministry confiscated Jewish wealth and property; the universities denied Jewish students admission and degrees while dismissing Jewish faculty; German industry fired Jewish workers, officers, board members and disenfranchised Jewish stockholders; government travel bureaus coordinated schedules and billing procedures for the railroads which carried the victims to their deaths.

"The process of extermination itself was bureaucratically systematic. Following the mob destruction of Kristallnacht, a pogrom in November 1938 in which at least 37 Jews were killed, 20,000 arrested, thousands of Jewish businesses looted and burned, and hundreds of synagogues vandalized, random acts of violence were replaced by organized, passionless operations. Similarly, the angry, riotous actions of the S.A. gave way to the disciplined, professional procedures of the nation for the earlier mobile killing units. The location and operation of the camps were based on calculations of accessibility and cost-effectiveness, the trademarks of modern business practice. German corporations actually profited from the industry of death. Pharmaceutical firms, unrestricted by fear of side effects, tested drugs on camp inmates, and companies competed for contracts to build ovens or supply gas for extermination. (Indeed, they were even concerned with protecting the patents for their products.) German engineers working for Topf and Sons supplied one camp alone with 46 ovens capable of burning 500 bodies an hour.

"Adjacent to the extermination camp at Auschwitz was a privately owned, corporately sponsored concentration camp called I. G. Auschwitz, a division of I. G. Farben. This multi-dimensional, petro-chemical complex brought human slavery to its ultimate perfection by reducing human beings to consumable raw materials, from which all mineral life was systematically drained before the bodies were recycled into the Nazi war economy; gold teeth for the treasury, hair for mattresses, ashes for fertilizer. In their relentless search for the least expensive and most efficient means of extermination, German scientists experimented with a variety of gasses until they discovered the insecticide Zyklon B, which could kill 2,000 persons in less than 30 minutes at a cost of one-half-cent per body. Near the end of the war, in order to cut expenses and save gas, "cost-accountant considerations" led to an order to place living children directly into the ovens or throw them into open burning pits. The same type of ingenuity and control that facilitates modern industrial development was rationally applied to the process of destruction.

"During previous centuries, excess populations were alleviated through emigration to less populated regions, but by 1920, the frontiers had receded and the New World no longer absorbed the overflow from the Old. When Germany could not ship out a population she wished to eliminate (no country was willing to accept Jew), she took the next fatal step and sent them up in smoke. In a world of increasing overpopulation, the inclination to duplicate the Nazi option and once again exterminate millions of people remains a hideous threat. The curse of the Holocaust is a dire warning.

"The Holocaust could not have occurred without the collapse of certain religious norms; increasing secularity fueled a devaluation of the image of the human being created in the likeness of God. Ironically, although religious perspectives contributed to the growth of anti-Semitism and the choice of Jews as victims, only in a modern secular age did anti-Semitism lead to annihilation. Other aspects of modern dehumanization contributed to the Holocaust, notably the splitting of the human personality whereby men could murder children by day and be loving husbands and fathers at night. The division of labor that separated complete operations into fractions of the whole permitted thousands to participate in a massive bureaucracy of death without feeling responsible. For example, Adolf Eichmann, who supervised the roundup of Jews for deportation, could claim he never personally killed a single person; employees could insist they did not know what they were doing; executioners could explain they were only following orders.

"Whether the product of technology or a reaction against it, the horror of the Holocaust is inextricably linked to the conditions of our time. By studying the Holocaust, we hope to help immunize modern man against the diseases particular to the twentieth century which led to this monstrous aberration." Pages 3-5

Lastly, in a Memorandum Decision and Order filed June 23, 1981, the United States District Court, Northern District of Ohio, Eastern Division, ordered the deportation of one John Demjanjuk on the grounds that he concealed his commission of atrocities against Jewish prisoners at the extermination camp of Treblinka. Among its findings of fact, the court held that:

"In 1942 the Nazis initiated 'Action Reinhard' in Poland, a codeword for the systematic extermination of the Jews from all the countries of Europe occupied by German forces." *US vs. John Demjanjuk*, C77-923.

"Those who cannot
remember the past are
condemned to repeat it."
GEORGE SANTAYNA,
The Life of Reason.

Dated: August 3, 1981
Respectfully submitted,
WILLIAM COX
Counsel for Plaintiff

(E) Supplemental Points and Authorities and Argument Regarding Corporate Liability

Liability of Corporation Legion for the Survival of Freedom for Contracts of Director

Under the law, "No limitation upon the business, purposes or powers of the corporation or upon the powers of the shareholders, officers or directors, or the manner of exercise of such powers" contained in the articles may be asserted "as between the corporation or any shareholder and any third person." (Corp. C 803(b).) A contract or conveyance made in the name of the corporation which is authorized or ratified by the directors, or is within the scope of their actual or apparent authority, binds the corporation and third persons, whether it is executed or executory. (Corp.C. 803(c).)

The Legion for the Survival of Freedom (LSF) is a Texas Corporation (see attachment 1). Its only corporate activity is doing business as the Noontide Press, The Independence House, and the Institute for Historical Review in Torrance, California (Elisabeth Carto deposition page 64) (attachment #2). While each publishes different types of books, [collectively] they are all one in the same (supra. page 65). According to the Comptroller of Public Accounts, state of Texas, in November 1980, the officers of the Legion for the Survival of Freedom were:

> Bruce Holmon—President-Director
> Lewis Furr—Vice President
> LaVonne Furr—Secretary-Director
> Elisabeth Carto—Treasurer
> (attachment #3)

In her deposition, Elisabeth Carto stated that between late 1979 and March 1981, LaVonne Furr had resigned as an officer and director in order to work on the *American Mercury* magazine which had been sold to Ned Touchstone. (page 84, 85). Mrs. Carto, who became both secretary and treasurer, never spoke to Mr. Holmon, Mr. Furr, or Mrs. Furr about corporate business during that same period (page 106). Mrs. Carto has no idea what transpired financially during that time (page 112) and was not consulted regarding the reward offer to plaintiff (page 93).

David McCalden was in charge of all operations of the Legion for the Survival of Freedom (Elisabeth Carto deposition page 86) and was relatively unsupervised (supra. page 87); however, to the extent that there was supervision, it was the responsibility of Elisabeth Carto (supra. page 88).

McCalden entered into an employment contract with the Legion for the Survival of Freedom on December 1, 1980, which was signed by Elisabeth Carto (see attachment 4). Except for salary, that contract was identical to the contract which governed his employment for the previous year (deposition of McCalden page 16-21).

That contract defines the duties of McCalden as follows: "The Employee agrees to devote his entire time and attention and all of his energy, abilities, talents, experience and contacts to the interests of the employer . . ."

It was McCalden who originally came up with the idea for the Institute for Historical Review (deposition of McCalden page 61). He consulted with Willis Carto (supra. page 62) with whom he met approximately three times weekly (supra. page 63) and left the more offensive, polemical, and subjective books with the Noontide Press (page 67), including the *Imperium*, the first title it ever printed (supra. page 70). The Institute for Historical Review was founded by money from the sale of [the] *American Mercury* [magazine] (supra. page 72).

The idea for the reward offer came after McCalden was instructed by Willis Carto, who made all major decisions (supra page 65), to contact Anthony Hilder, a Hollywood Public Relations person and director of Liberty Life (supra. page 82). McCalden then presented the idea to Carto who approved its offer (supra. page 84). McCalden thought they might get a "few naive zealots" to apply; however, the plaintiff's acceptance "was the first proper claim" (supra. page 85).

McCalden confirms that Elisabeth Carto had little to do with policy decisions, and that neither she nor Holmon or the Furrs were specifically contacted regarding the offer (supra. page 86, 87). Her role was to relay information to and from Willis Carto (supra. page 87).

McCalden first became aware of Mel Mermelstein from a clipping from the *Jerusalem Post* (supra. page 87). His mailing of the "put up or shut up" letter to the plaintiff was within his authority as being "in charge of the office" (supra. page 91). He had previously mailed out approximately 30 such letters, as "obviously I was in charge of publicity and public relations, I was authorized to take whatever steps I thought were appropriate to make the reward a success" (supra. page 92). He stated that on an ongoing basis he would from time to time discuss with

Willis Carto that he was sending out letters and that no one was accepting the offer (supra. page 92). Specifically, he felt that he had the authority to bind the corporation and that the making of the offer was fully within his authority (supra. page 94).

Plaintiff's acceptance was the only claim that met the threshold requirements and the only thing left remaining would be to submit to the tribunal of experts (supra. page 96). However, after receiving that claim, a similar letter was mailed to Simon Wiesenthal, who responded prior to the defendant's letter to plaintiff on January 27, 1981, in which he was notified that his claim would be dealt with "later" (supra. pages 96,97) (see attachment 5).

The Legion for the Survival of Freedom intended to first deal with a claim from Wiesenthal at its 1981 conference in November (supra. page 97). While no firm plans had been made for the 1982 conference it was tentatively planned for the summer of 1982 (supra. pages 99,100). While there was some discussion with Willis Carto about having an earlier special tribunal to deal with plaintiff's claim (supra. page 99), there was never any correspondence with plaintiff on the subject (supra. page 100).

Thus, at the time the lawsuit was filed on February 19, 1981, it was within the reasonable expectation of the plaintiff that he would likely have to wait until summer 1982 to present his evidence, even though McCalden in deposition stated that the requirement that plaintiff answer *"very soon"* would have been a *one month* period (supra. page 100), in spite of the plaintiff's first mailing in December having contained everything necessary to get plaintiff past the threshold question (supra. page 101). Plaintiff's demand that the threshold question be resolved in an equally timely manner was deemed unreasonable by McCalden (supra. pages 101, 102).

The motive for the Legion for the Survival of Freedom to offer the reward was to increase publicity and to communicate with more people (supra. page 121) and that motive succeeded in gaining "a great deal of publicity." However, McCalden admitted that it was a "gimmick," that defendant didn't believe that any reward was going to be paid, and that they only "spent 15 cents mailing a letter to Mel Mermelstein" (supra. page 120). It is interesting to note that April 1981 was one of the Institute's "better months," deriving $30,000 in revenue (supra. page 121).

Prior to the time the lawsuit was filed, McCalden had many discussions with Willis Carto. During none of these discussions was it specifically complained of that McCalden exceeded his authority in sending the letter to the plaintiff (supra. page 132). It was only after the lawsuit was filed that Carto complained that "the $50,000 reward had expired and that reopening it had brought about a lot of different problems for the office" (supra. page 133). The primary source of discontent leading to the firing of McCalden was his refusal to turn up at the Institute for Historical Review office on a Sunday when the Jewish Defense League was demonstrating, and during which Willis Carto was assaulted (supra. page 133).

Any question about whether McCalden was authorized to make the offer on behalf of the corporation was laid to rest by the following questions asked of McCalden by counsel for the defense during the deposition:

> "Question: You were actually working, you were doing all of this, upon instructions of the corporation, is that right?
>
> "Answer: Yes, I was" (supra. page 182).

Liability of Corporation Legion for the Survival of Freedom for Torts

A corporation is ordinarily liable under the doctrine of *respondent superior* for torts of its agents or employees committed while they are acting within the scope of their employment. It is immaterial that the particular act was not authorized or ratified, or that it was *ultra vires*. (*Chamberlain vs. California Edison Company* (1914) 167 C. 500, 506, 140 P.25; *Hiroshima vs. Pac. G. & E. Co.* (1936) 18 C.A.2d 24, 31, 63 P.2d 340; *Maynard vs. Fireman's Fund Ins. Co.* (1867) 34 C. 48, 56; see 2 Cal. L. Rev. 410; 18 A.L.R.2d 402, 414; 55 A.L.R.2d 828; 19 Am.Jur.2d, Corporations Section 1427; BAJI (5th ed.) No. 13.30; Corporations.)

A corporation may also be held liable for exemplary damages where its agents, in committing a wrong, are guilty of malice or oppression. (*Lowe vs. Yolo etc. Water Co.* (1910) 157 C. 503, 510, 108 P. 297; see 13 So. Cal. L. Rev. 140; infra, Sec. 857.)

> (a) In an action for the breach of an obligation not arising from contract, where the defendant has been guilty of oppression, fraud, or malice, the plaintiff, in addition to

the actual damages, may recover damages for the sake of example and by way of punishing the defendant.

(b) An employer shall not be liable for damages pursuant to subdivision (a), based upon acts of an employee of the employer, unless the employer had advance knowledge of the unfitness of the employee and employed him or her with a conscious disregard of the rights or safety of others or authorized or ratified the wrongful conduct for which the damages are awarded or was personally guilty of oppression, fraud, or malice. With respect to a corporate employer, the advance knowledge, ratification, or act of oppression, fraud, or malice must be on the part of an officer, director, or managing agent of the corporation.

(c) As used in this section, the following definitions shall apply:

> (1) "Malice" means conduct which is intended by the defendant to cause injury to the plaintiff or conduct which is carried on by the defendant with a conscious disregard of the rights or safety of others.
>
> (2) "Oppression" means subjecting a person to cruel and unjust hardship in conscious disregard of that person's rights.
>
> (3) "Fraud" means an intentional misrepresentation, deceit, or concealment of a material fact known to the defendant with the intention on the part of the defendant of thereby depriving a person of property or legal rights or otherwise causing injury.

(Civil Code Sec. 3294)

The question thus becomes whether the Legion for the Survival of Freedom had:

(1) advance knowledge of the unfitness of the employee, or

(2) employed him with a conscious disregard of the rights or safety of others, or

(3) authorized or ratified the wrongful conduct for which the damages are awarded, or

(4) was personally guilty of oppression, fraud, or malice, and

(5) with respect to the corporate employer, the advance knowledge, ratification, or act of oppression, fraud, or malice must be on the part of an officer, director, or managing agent of the corporation.

As to the first and second questions, while McCalden refused during his deposition to answer questions regarding his employment prior to the Legion for the Survival of Freedom (deposition of McCalden pages 47-50), the *Los Angeles Times* in an article dated May 3, 1981 (heretofore attached to declaration by counsel for plaintiff dated May 5, 1981) identifies McCalden as "a writer and editor of allegedly racist and anti-Semitic publications in England before he came to this country as a 'permanent resident alien' in 1978." The article went on to report that McCalden was "a neo-fascist activist who defected from the National Front in 1975 to help form the National Party, a group that espoused 'British racial nationalism'." McCalden was reported to have said, "I believe in writing material which encourages race discrimination because I am a racialist."

It is thus clear that the defendant Legion for the Survival of Freedom either ignored the past racist activities of McCalden, or else those activities were qualifications for the position, as McCalden went on in the same article to say that the "Noontide Press puts out books of a very conservative nature," including some that "are anti-Semitic."

As to whether the corporation authorized or ratified the acts of McCalden in challenging the plaintiff, it has already been established that he was directed by Willis Carto to consult with Hilder, who created the reward idea, and subsequently to publish the offer. Further, for a period of time, Willis Carto ratified the act through discussions until such time as a lawsuit was filed. Even thereafter, it was at the direction of Willis Carto that a letter was sent to plaintiff directing him to appear at the November 1980 conference to present his evidence. It was only after McCalden refused to show up at a demonstration that he was fired.

As to actual malice, it can either be express or implied and may be inferred from the facts of the case. As was established above, the motive of the defendant was to create greater media coverage of its efforts to prove that the Holocaust did not occur. That such a contention would cause harm or grief to one who had been a victim is confirmed by McCalden. In his deposition, while steadfastly refusing to admit that even one Jew might have been gassed at Auschwitz, (supra. pages 243, 144), he admitted that the camp was the "anus mundi" in the summer of 1944 (supra. page 117), that Jews were executed there (supra. page 144), that he would not dispute that Jews were killed by phenol injections or by gas lorries (supra. pages 146, 147), and that he was open to the idea "that euthanasia was practiced" (supra. page 157). He admitted that 50,000 pounds of Zyclon B gas was provided to Auschwitz during 1942 and 1943 alone; however, he was unwilling to admit that the plaintiff may have been traumatized by his experience there (supra page 119).

McCalden, however, had no information or evidence to offer which might contradict plaintiff's declaration except that it appeared that a photograph may have been retouched (supra. pages 136, 139). Moreover, the current director of the Institute for Historical Review, Thomas Marcellus, stated during his deposition that he knew of no evidence to the contrary except for his belief that its five crematoriums could not burn fast enough the reported numbers (page 68). Elisabeth Carto in her deposition refused to relate any evidence that the plaintiff did not suffer gravely from his experiences (pages 184-187).

The final question then becomes whether McCalden was acting as the director and/or managing agent of the corporation. As has been shown above, he was in charge of the day-to-day operation of the corporation activities, and, in addition, all formal supervising, if any, came from Elisabeth Carto.

In order to determine the corporation's own motives, it is necessary to examine who, if anyone, actually directed his activities. Any objective analysis identifies the person of Willis Carto as the prime manipulator.

Role of Willis Carto in the Operation of the Legion for the Survival of Freedom

The Legion was incorporated on April 14, 1952, by Frances Whalen Clark, Jason Matthews, and Marcia C. J. Matthews in the state of Texas to do a general advertising business in "aiding and assisting in the promotion and preservation of American Constitutional Government . . . and to conduct publicity campaigns designed to educate the American Public in the fundamentals of Americanism" (attachment #1). According to Elisabeth Carto, Jason Matthews was formerly the publisher of *American Mercury* and is now deceased (deposition page 56).

A report filed with the state of Texas on March 1, 1965 shows the officers to be:

> Marcia J. Hoyt - President
> LaVonne Furr - Vice President
> Edwin A. Walker - Secretary-Treasurer
> (attachment #3)

On June 30, 1966, articles of merger were filed with the state of Texas, blending into the Legion a Washington, DC corporation known as the Committee for Religious Development. The document was signed by Willis Carto on behalf of the Legion for the Survival of Freedom as vice president. Among the debts assumed by the Legion were six notes to W. A. Carto on demand in the amount of $22,871.15 (attachment #1).

In the tax records heretofore marked as attachment 3, W. A. Carto is listed as the treasurer in the report filed for the tax year 1969. Thereafter, his name does not appear; however, his wife continued to serve as an officer.

In determining the role of Willis Carto in the operation of the Legion for the Survival of Freedom, it is instructive to again look to the deposition of McCalden. Employment was first sought by McCalden who called the Noontide Press from England (deposition of McCalden page 23). He first spoke with LaVonne Furr who handed the phone to Willis Carto (supra. page 24). McCalden was hired during a personal interview with Willis Carto in Torrance, California (supra. page 25).

All major decisions were made by Willis Carto (supra. page 65), including the founding of the Institute for Historical Review (supra. page 70) and the original making of the offer (supra. page 84). When the acceptance by Mermelstein was received, McCalden immediately consulted Willis Carto:

> "Q. You mailed a letter . . . in January in which you stated you were consulting with the committee, is that true?

A. I believe that is true.

Q. And to what committee were you referring to?

A. The Corporation of the Legion.

Q. And who would that have been?

A. It would have been Willis Carto, who was talking as the agent of the corporation and their business consultant.

Q. And what did you say and what did he say?

A. I said that we had a claim for the reward or what appeared to be a claim, and I asked for his instructions.

Q. What did he tell you?

A. He said "hold everything until I get back there."

Finally, it was Willis Carto who fired McCalden:

Q. Did you have a discussion with Willis Carto regarding your resignation?

A. Yes I did.

Q. Did he indicate to you that it might be best if you terminated your services to the corporation?

A. He gave me his memorandum in his capacity as agent for the corporation, which stated that the termination clause in my contract was being instituted and that I had five days to consider my position (supra. pages 129, 130).

That memorandum was subsequently destroyed by McCalden (supra. page 130); however, his resignation was personally handed to Willis Carto (supra. page 131).

The letter sent to plaintiff following service of the lawsuit in which plaintiff was invited to present his evidence in November 1981 was sent at the direction of Willis Carto (supra. page 187).

Finally, McCalden stated that Willis Carto "had the authority vested in him by the corporation to oversee the administration of projects such as this one" (supra. page 188).

The Motives of Willis Carto Can Form the Basis of Malice on Behalf of the Legion for the Survival of Freedom

"In order to justify an award of exemplary damages, the defendant must be guilty of oppression, fraud, or malice. He must act with the intent to vex, injure, or annoy, or with a conscious disregard of the plaintiff's rights. Defendant's requisite state of mind may be proved either expressly by direct evidence probative on the existence of hatred or ill will or by implication through indirect evidence from which the jury may draw inferences." *Neal vs. Farmers Insurance Exchange* (1978) 21 C. 3d 910, 148 Cal. Rptr. 389.

While the motivation behind the reward offer to plaintiff has been established above as a "gimmick" to obtain publicity, it is necessary to look further in order to learn the reason behind the motive. Thus, the manner in which that publicity would serve Willis Carto and his wholly controlled Legion for the Survival of Freedom becomes controlling.

To look into the mind of Willis Carto is, of course, impossible; however, from his introduction to the *Imperium*, we can learn much as an analysis of that publication shows that Carto sees his media empire as a means of obtaining political power in order to effectuate his policies of racism. Quoting the final paragraph of that analysis, we can perhaps see the reason why the plaintiff was selected.

> "While future historians may define Yockey's work as only the bizarre observations of a misguided seer, the political implications of Carto's interpretation raise these beliefs to a new highly dangerous level and must be seen for the incendiary they are. For if the *Journal for Historical Review* (heretofore reviewed in a previous declaration) is an example of Carto's 'words-in-action', then we may be seeing in his views the rising of the same kind of 'Big Lie' propaganda that fueled the fire of Nazism in the Third Reich. From the reading, it would seem that Carto would push the extent of his First Amendment privileges of free speech to its utmost limit, stopping barely short of advocating the violent overthrow of our legitimately established and democratic government, to the extent that such government prevents the effectuation of his prophetic policies." (attachment 6)

[Paragraphs omitted]

Again in 1971, *The National Review* attempted to define the extent of Carto's empire:

> "Today eleven years later, Carto presides over a business empire with annual receipts of at least a million dollars. His operations include publication of books, pamphlets and periodicals, direct-mail solicitation, campaign financing, fund-raising, a little travel agency and data processing on the side. He is the man behind such respectable-sounding organizations as Liberty Lobby, United Congressional Appeal, Save Our Schools, Americans for National Security, the *Washington Observer*, the *American Mercury*. Notwithstanding that these organizations affect a concern for American values and constitutionalism, Carto is driven by a philosophy of pure power, a philosophy essentially alien and fundamentally hostile to the American tradition, the philosophy of Yockey."

Carto's battle "for a better America" takes many forms. Perhaps the most destructive was his publication through the Noontide Press of the *White Student*, a KKK type flier designed to be distributed to high school students. With titles such as "We Want White Studies," "Stop the Buses," "Bleak Prospects for White Graduates," "Roots to be Renamed Hoots," and "Race the Nation," it also offered for sale a complete selection of "Race Survival Books." (see attachment 9)

Carto's search for power takes many other forms as well. In a circular dated August 8, 1980, Carto is pictured as a Will Rogers look alike encouraging people to "save America from . . . anarchy and dictatorship" by subscribing to and peddling the "Liberty Letter." (see attachment 10)

The Damage Done to Plaintiff Has Been Both Real and Extreme

The damage done to plaintiff must be seen as two parts of the same whole. First, unless one were to have personally experienced the unspeakable horror of Auschwitz during that terrible summer of 1944 during which at least 10,000 persons were murdered every single day, one cannot imagine the wave of emotion that swept over the plaintiff as he was forced to read the revolting words written in the offer letter which called his memories a lie.

Secondly, unless one were Jewish in our contemporary society, one cannot understand the agony of decision in deciding whether or not to accept the offer. To ignore the challenge leaves until another day the cleaning of the barn until such time as the odor becomes overbearing and the manure overflows into the yard. To accept means exposing the plaintiff to having to appear at defendant's kangaroo court and suffer the humiliation of proving one's case "beyond a shadow of a doubt" to a group of biased bigots, thereby providing them the publicity they so ardently desired.

The plaintiff had no choice; having once witnessed the incredibly horrible result of Hitler's racist philosophy now shared by Carto, he could not sit idly by and allow it to happen again. Then, having made their devil's bargain, the defendants' immediately breached it in favor of a more desirable "mouse" to play with. (see attachment 11)

Plaintiff then had no choice but to go to law in order to obtain justice; however, his pain and that of his family has continued. As can be readily seen from the declaration of Dr. William Vicary, the letter and its sequela has had a devastating effect upon the mental health of the plaintiff:

> "Noteworthy during my interviews with the plaintiff and his family was the fact that they tended to minimize their difficulties as a result of the events beginning with the letter. This derives from several reasons. First, the plaintiff and his family share a pattern of intellectualizing or rationalizing problems as opposed to ventilating the underlying feelings. Second, they are realistically cautious with strangers given the adversity which they have suffered over the past many months. Third, they are fearful that expressing their intimate problems in the litigation will result in public disclosure and humiliation. Nevertheless, I was able to gain some appreciation of the difficulties that they have endured over the past several months. For example, despite his intelligent narration and brave appearance, the plaintiff was frequently on the verge of tears during both interviews.

"Even with the resolution of the litigation, it will probably be a substantial period of time before the plaintiff and his family recover from the pain and suffering that they have experienced. If the plaintiff does not achieve some form of moral triumph or other victory through the litigation, it is likely that his anguish as a result of the letter and its sequela will smolder for the indefinite future. Even as resilient and resourceful an individual as the plaintiff has human limits as to the amount of agony and despair that can be successfully coped with." (attachment 12)

Conclusion

The assault against plaintiff has continued throughout the lawsuit thus far. Recently, the editor of the *Press Telegram* received another "Jewish Information Bulletin" in which a cartoon is labeled "Mel Mermelstein - The Trial of a Nut." The material is signed by David Cohen, who Marcellus during his deposition identified as Felderer. (see attachment 13)

On July 13, 1981 the *Spotlight* newspaper carried an article entitled "Exterminationist Refuses Offer Reward from Revisionists." The article alleges that "Mel Mermelstein, peripatetic Holocaust witness, has refused a continuing offer by the Institute for Historical Review (IHR) to consider his claim for the $50,000 reward offered by the Institute to the first person who can prove that Jews were gassed in gas chambers at Auschwitz." (see attachment 14)

At the same time, the defendants continue to refuse to participate in meaningful discovery. Although Mermelstein answered hundreds of questions during a five-hour deposition, including many that were plainly degrading, Elisabeth Carto and McCalden refused to answer dozens and dozens of clearly relevant questions, particularly those designed to establish their true identity (refer to copies of depositions heretofore filed with the court in connection with plaintiff's motion to continue).

On June 26, 1981, defendant Legion for the Survival of Freedom refused to supply a corporate representative to appear and to produce documents. Counsel for defendant did appear and produced a copy of McCalden's employment contract and his memorandum of resignation;

however, many relevant documents were not produced. (see attachment 15)

There is no reason to believe that there will be greater cooperation in the future. Recently, a lawsuit brought by Liberty Lobby against the Anti-Defamation League was dismissed when Willis Carto refused to appear at an ordered oral examination. However, he used very aggressive discovery methods to ransack the files of the Anti-Defamation League before allowing the suit to be dismissed. The information garnered was then used to publish a "White Paper" calling for the registration of the Anti-Defamation League as an agent for a foreign power, Israel. (see attachment 16)

It thus seems critical that this matter be resolved as quickly as possible. To ask plaintiff to continue alone against Carto's empire during protracted litigation is to ask the impossible. Not only does his suffering continue, but the weeds of racism sown by Carto will continue to spread throughout his forest of deceit.

At the time plaintiff filed for hearing on default judgment against defendant Legion for the Survival of Freedom on June 3, 1981, it was noted that plaintiff sought only damages in the amount of $50,000 plus costs. At that hearing, the plaintiff having to suffer through the agonizing five hour deposition, defendants were put on notice of a settlement offer of $100,000 plus costs up to the time of hearing on motion for summary judgment. (see attachment 17)

As can be seen from above, the assault has continued and it is now prayed that the court will find damages in the amount of $1,050,000 and award costs of litigation. Anything less will likely be ineffectual in stopping the assault and repaying the plaintiff for his suffering.

Dated: August 10, 1981

WILLIAM COX, Attorney for Plaintiff

(F) Motion to Strike Signature of Complaint Pursuant to Rule 11

In the United States District Court
for the District of Columbia
Willis A. Carto, Plaintiff, versus
William J. Cox, et al., Defendants
Civil Action #83-1788

COMES NOW the Defendant, William J. Cox, *in pro per*, and pursuant to Rule 11 of the Federal Rules of Civil Procedure moves for the striking of the signature from the complaint.

1. The bringing of the complaint involved wrongful motivation of the plaintiff to the extent that it constitutes a fraud upon the Court and a criminal contempt of its dignity and purpose.

2. Counsel for the plaintiff does not enjoy the independence normally expected of an officer of the Court in that he is an employee of the plaintiff, he serves in a subaltern role, does the express wrongful bidding of his client, and conducted no independent investigation of the circumstances before filing the instant complaint.

WHEREFORE, Defendant prays that the signature of counsel for the plaintiff be stricken from the complaint.

WILLIAM J. COX, *in pro per*

Memorandum of Points and Authorities in Support of Motion to Strike Signature

1. Prior to changes made in the Federal Rules of Civil Procedure and in the practices of most state courts, plaintiffs were required to personally sign and verify the contents of their civil complaints. Under existing rules, counsel for the plaintiff may sign the complaint. However, Rule 11 provides that the signature may be stricken if a sham or false.

> Rule 11—Signing of Pleading

> "...If a pleading is not signed or is signed with intent to defeat the purpose of this rule, it may be stricken as sham and false and the action may proceed as though the pleading had not been signed. For a willful violation of this rule an attorney may be subjected to appropriate disciplinary action. Similar action may be taken if scandalous or indecent matter is inserted."

2. There were two complaints filed in the instant case. The first was signed on June 16, 1983 and the second on July 12, 1983. The only substantial difference is that the second strikes any reference to the Jewish Defense League or its officers. Both complaints bear the purported signature of Fleming Lee; however, an examination reveals apparent differences in the signatures. Defendant does not know which, if either, signature is by counsel for the plaintiff.

3. Given the fact that counsel for plaintiff is the General Counsel of the Liberty Lobby, an organization in which plaintiff Willis Carto is the Treasurer and acknowledged leader, that Mr. Lee serves as a full-time employee under the personal direction and control of the plaintiff, and that Mr. Lee has failed to demonstrate the requisite independence expected of an officer of the court, it is clear that the signature, if indeed that of Mr. Lee, does not contain any assurance to the court or defendants regarding the verification of the contents of said complaint.

4. On a number of occasions in the past, the plaintiff has filed complaints against those people or organizations that he considers to be political enemies. These complaints have been dismissed when Willis Carto refused to participate in discovery. At the same time, he obtains information which is either printed out of context by his publishing organizations or is used as the basis of further legal harassment. For example, Carto sued Jack Anderson over an article that Anderson published in his *Investigator* magazine. Defendant Cox was deposed in

that suit before it was dismissed against Carto without his personally having to be deposed. Information from Cox's deposition is now used to make out a conspiracy fantasy in the present lawsuit.

5. In the investigation of Carto and his organizations, defendant Cox contacted hundreds of individuals and organizations seeking information. This was made necessary by the secrecy and misdealing of the plaintiff Carto. To now be made subject to a lawsuit in a forum 3,000 miles from his home, in which he will have to contend with intrusive interrogatories and questioning about many matters that are privileged and to have to argue each such intrusion would constitute for him an overwhelming constitutional deprivation of due process and equal protection of law.

6. This attempt by the plaintiff to pervert the justice system to his own unworthy purposes is so blatant and wrong as to constitute a criminal contempt.

Power of Court

"A court of the United States shall have the power to punish by fine or imprisonment, at its discretion, such contempt of its authority, and none other, as (1) misbehavior of any person in its presence or so near thereto as to obstruct the administration of justice."

Title 18 USC Section 401

7. It is urged that the Court inquire of counsel for the plaintiff regarding his participation in this fraud, and to order the plaintiff to show cause why the signature of counsel should not be stricken and the entire matter referred to the Justice Department for investigation.

WILLIAM J. COX, *in pro per*

DECLARATION IN SUPPORT OF MOTION TO STRIKE SIGNATURE

1. I, William J. Cox, do hereby declare and state that what follows is true and correct to the best of my knowledge and belief.

2. My declaration made in connection with the motion to dismiss under rule 12(b) is hereby incorporated as a part of this declaration as though fully set forth herein.

3. My investigation of Willis Carto made in connection with the Los Angeles lawsuit clearly places him in direct control of at least three separate groups of organizations. The first is the Legion for the Survival of Freedom, which does business in Torrance, California under the name of the Institute for Historical Review, the Noontide Press, and Independence House. This group is primarily a publishing operation which supplies the radical rightwing of America with some of the most racist, anti-American, and anti-Christian literature available. Some of the material published is such that it can only be compared with pornography in which children are used as actors. The publications appeal to those who hate and would destroy democracy as we know it, and who would kill and enslave those who disagree with Carto or those who by virtue of their birth are not of the great Germanic race that he worships.

4. The next organization controlled by Carto is the Liberty Lifeline Foundation, formerly known as the Council on Dangerous Drugs. By having access to those who inquire regarding a trust manual sold by Independence House, elderly Americans are convinced to leave their estates, in trust, in situations where the money is ultimately funneled to the Liberty Lobby.

5. Another organizational structure totally controlled by Carto is the Liberty Lobby and those other related organizations such as *The Spotlight* newspaper, which occupies the same office space at 300 Independence Avenue in Washington, DC. These organizations also include a political action committee which channels money to influence the actions of Congress. However, a check of public records reveals no accounting for the vast funds accumulated by these organizations.

6. Through various associations, Carto is also involved in the organized Ku Klux Klan and Nazi movements in America, the organized tax revolt, and those who accumulate private arsenals.

7. The headquarters of the Liberty Lobby at 300 Independence Avenue is an old, converted mansion connected by a rabbit warren of passages to other buildings adjacent to the east. Within these confines, Willis Carto is the virtual dictator, making all decisions and directing all operations. Counsel for Willis Carto in this action, Fleming Lee, is the general counsel of the Liberty Lobby, and in that role, works directly for and under the supervision of Willis Carto. Given the bunker mentality that exists there, Mr. Lee would be fired if he disagreed with Mr. Carto.

8. On May 21, 1981, when Mr. Carto did not appear as directed for deposition, I called him in Washington, DC, and my call was referred to Mr. Lee. I was informed by Mr. Lee that he did not represent Mr. Carto. On a previous occasion when I was in Washington, I attempted to call Mr. Carto and my call was also directed to Mr. Lee. I was informed at that time by Mr. Lee that Mr. Carto was in California. This statement was suspect, as I had information from my investigators which placed Mr. Carto in Washington on that same date.

9. The evil motives of Mr. Carto can most readily be established by a thorough reading of his introduction to the *Imperium*, in which he implicitly acknowledges having a role in the death of Francis Parker Yockey on June 16, 1960. In the twisted mind of Willis Carto, the spirit of Yockey occupied his body, and he became the living embodiment of Adolf Hitler, to whom the *Imperium* is dedicated as "the hero of the Second World War."

10. The trail of death and violence that attends the actions of Willis Carto is next marked in 1966 when he took over the Legion for the Survival of Freedom which was then controlled by General Edwin Walker. The retired general had been the victim of an attempted assassination three years earlier by Lee Harvey Oswald on April 10, 1963 in Dallas, Texas. It is interesting to note that the meeting of directors, during which the takeover was effected at a time when Willis Carto was the vice-president of that organization, was on June 16, 1966, the sixth anniversary of the death of Yockey.

11. In later years, we find Carto again involved in an organizational takeover. This time the organization was Youth for Wallace, the predecessor organization of the National Youth Alliance. While Carto's control of the Alliance was not lasting, the attempted assassination of George Wallace, a presidential candidate at the same time, cannot be ignored.

12. Lastly, on the 23rd anniversary of Yockey's death, we have the signing on June 16, 1983 of the first complaint in the instant case. That this date was selected for the initiation of this irrational action cannot be a coincidence.

13. Willis Carto is a dangerous man. Given his devotion to establishing on the American continent an imperium based upon the tenets of "Absolute Socialism," he is an enemy of freedom and democracy. His belief in the power of propaganda, and his hatred of those who he labels as "culture distorters," causes him to engage in a new, great lie that the Jews were not the victims of Nazi genocide, that it was a figment of their imagination. The propagation of such a horrendous lie makes suspect each and every statement made by Carto and those who do his bidding. It is because history teaches us that such beliefs led to a great war in which some thirty million persons died within our lifetime, that I did what I did [in pursuing this case], and now, as best I can, answer this latest assault by those who embrace the philosophy that all men and women are not equal before the law.

August 31, 1983

WILLIAM J. COX, *in pro per*

(G) MOTION TO DISMISS UNDER RULE 12(B)

In the United States District Court
for the District of Columbia
Willis A. Carto, Plaintiff, versus
William J. Cox, et al., Defendants
Civil Action #83-1788

COMES NOW the Defendant, William J. Cox, *in pro per*, pursuant to Rule 12(b) of the Federal Rules of Procedure, moving for a dismissal of this action and for costs and counsel fees and as reasons therefore states that:

1. This Court has no personal jurisdiction over the defendant.

2. The proper venue for this action is not the District of Columbia.

3. This action was filed by Plaintiff with full knowledge that said jurisdiction does not exist, and with the purpose of avoiding justice in a pending action in the Superior Court of the State of California.

4. Alternatively, the applicable Statute of Limitations in California bars the complaint herein.

WHEREFORE, Defendant prays that the case be dismissed, with costs and counsel fees awarded, and Defendant has attached a Memorandum of Points and Authorities which he prays shall be read as a part hereof.

August 31, 1983

WILLIAM J. COX, *in pro per*

Memorandum of Points and Authorities in Support of Defendant's Motion to Dismiss

1. Defendant William J. Cox adopts the points, authorities, and arguments advanced by co-defendants Mermelstein and Brin in their Motion to Dismiss dated July 13, 1983 as though fully set forth herein.

2. This cause of action should be barred because the plaintiff Willis Carto is a *de facto* defendant in a California lawsuit which provides him an adequate forum to seek redress should he feel offended. He is a *de facto* defendant because he personally retained counsel for and directed the defense of that case, because he personally submitted and signed a declaration in that case and because he has willfully avoided personal service in that case.

3. In the alternative, Willis Carto is a fugitive from jurisdiction in that case, having removed himself and his primary assets from the jurisdiction and has willfully failed to participate, as ordered, in discovery in that case.

4. Plaintiff asserts that venue in the District of Columbia is appropriate "in that an important part of the claim arose in the District of Columbia, if for no other reason that defendant Cox's contacts there with agents of columnist Jack Anderson." However, Cox was never named as a defendant in the lawsuit brought by plaintiff against Jack Anderson, even though he appeared as requested by plaintiff at a deposition. That case was dismissed as have been others where plaintiff initiates court action and then refuses to participate in meaningful discovery.

5. The defendant has no assets, residence, property or business whatever in the District of Columbia. His only contacts in the District during the period of time in question related only to conducting an investigation of Willis Carto after the plaintiff had fled from the jurisdiction of the Los Angeles Court. The only personal contact with the plaintiff involved having him served on the city streets with a notice to appear at a deposition, which he failed to do.

6. Without waiving any jurisdictional issue, it is also clear that the one year statute of limitation on most torts in California clearly applies as an alternative in seeking dismissal of this case. All acts relative to this matter occurred prior to October 1981 at which time the Superior Court ruled against all defendants in Los Angeles and all contacts in Washington, DC ceased.

7. As will be taken up in more detail in the motion under Rule 11, the bringing of this complaint is in complete violation of the jurisdictional rules of the Court, under conditions designed to serve the questionable objectives of the plaintiff constitute a criminal contempt of the dignity of the Court. For that reason, costs of this defense therefore are requested.

August 31, 1983

WILLIAM J. COX, *in pro per*

DECLARATION IN SUPPORT OF MOTION TO DISMISS

1. I, William J. Cox, do hereby declare and state that what follows is true and correct to the best of my knowledge and belief.

2. I am an attorney and counselor at law, licensed by the State of California and admitted to practice before all courts of this state and before the United States District Court, Central District, of the State of California.

3. Between the years 1977 and 1982, I operated a private practice in the City of Long Beach as an investigative lawyer, working primarily in the criminal law, handling a large number of *pro bono* cases in matters where the need existed, specializing in the defense of juvenile offenders, and experimenting with the concept of dispute mediation as an alternative to civil litigation.

4. My qualifications as a professional counselor and investigative lawyer include 20 years' experience in the criminal justice field including service as a police officer, prosecutor, defense counsel, and judge *pro tempore* in three judicial districts. Moreover, I was employed by the US Justice Department as a police expert and administrator, having authored the current "Policy Manual" of the Los Angeles Police Department and the introductory chapters regarding the role of the police in America for the Police Task Force of the National Advisory Commission on Criminal Justice Standards and Goals.

5. What follows is a chronological reconstruction of the facts that appear relevant to the complaint which has been filed in the instant case. In making this Declaration, I waive no privileges, nor do I submit to the jurisdiction of the Court.

6. On or about November 28, 1980, I was contacted by Mel Mermelstein, a local Long Beach businessman who had written a book about his experiences as a survivor of several Nazi death camps, including Auschwitz.

7. Mr. Mermelstein had received a letter signed by the director, Louis Brandon, of the Institute for Historical Review (IHR) in which Mr. Mermelstein was told that it was understood that he could prove that the Holocaust occurred and that if no response was forthcoming, that his refusal to so prove would be publicized.

8. Mr. Mermelstein was very upset, emotionally and physically, by his receipt of that letter and almost simultaneously by one received from Sweden written by Ditleib Felderer, in which a number of libelous statements were made.

9. I conducted a limited investigation in which it was determined that the IHR was licensed to do business in Torrance, California, along with the Noontide Press and Independence House under the Legion for the Survival of Freedom, a Texas-based corporation. The officer of the corporation who signed the business license application was Elisabeth Carto, the wife of the plaintiff. The investigation also showed that Ditleib Felderer was a member of the Advisory Committee of the IHR.

10. My review of the facts indicated that while the Felderer letter was clearly actionable as a libel, the IHR letter was a far more subtle device to discredit and embarrass Mermelstein. If the IHR letter were answered, it would place him in a position where a fair and impartial review would be virtually impossible without court supervision, and if he refused to answer, his refusal would be publicized as a failure to so prove.

11. It was decided to fully and completely answer the letter and to accept the offer, providing in the return a complete statement of Mermelstein, whose testimony as an eyewitness would be sufficient under California law to prove or disprove any disputed fact.

12. I then accepted employment as counsel for the plaintiff in what was to become widely known as "The Holocaust Case" on a *pro bono* basis. That employment was to last for over one and a half years, during which time a lengthy and complete investigation of the activities of Willis Carto and his various organizations was conducted, legal actions were brought against those organizations which most contributed to the injuries caused Mermelstein, and various rulings were obtained which favored those filings. During most of that time, I worked virtually full

time on the Holocaust Case, to the detriment of my remaining practice, and I advanced unreimbursed costs of approximately $40,000.

13. Following an exchange of correspondence with the IHR, we were informed that the hearing of Mermelstein's case was to be delayed until sometime in the future, as it had been determined to first review a later claim made by Simon Wiesenthal, who the IRH labeled in one of its publications as a "most eminently suitable mouse" in its "publicity gimmick."

14. On February 19, 1981, a complaint was filed in the Superior Court of the County of Los Angeles in which it was alleged that the defendants, including the Legion for the Survival of Freedom, its satellite organizations, its officers and its director harmed Mermelstein by breach or anticipatory breach of contract, libel, intentional infliction of emotional distress, and injurious denial of an established fact. The complaint prayed for summary relief as well.

15. Further investigation revealed that the IHR operated out of a storefront in an industrial area of Torrance, that its doors were kept locked, and that no sign was displayed outside. It was further learned that the true name of the director, Louis Brandon, was in fact David McCalden.

16. Attempts to personally serve the complaint were unsuccessful until March 17, 1981, when David McCalden was personally served, and on March 20, 1981, when Elisabeth Carto was personally served on her behalf and on behalf of the corporation. More complete details regarding this phase of the investigation is contained in the documents filed in connection with the subsequent default hearing which are include in the Memorandum of Information contained in Defendant's Motion for Judicial Notice, under tab 1. (MJN #1)

17. On April 21, 1981, when no answer had been filed and no correspondence or telephonic communication had been received, a default judgment was filed with the court. (MJN #2)

18. In the meantime, attempts to obtain discovery facts from the defendants were frustrated by their refusal to accept any mail bearing the return address of my law office. Moreover, on May 6, 1981, David McCalden failed to appear for a scheduled deposition in my office, and on May 7, 1981, Elisabeth Carto failed to make a similar appearance.

19. During the month of May 1981, my attempts to obtain background information regarding the various named defendants were

stymied due to a lack of cooperation from various Jewish organizations, such as the Anti-Defamation League and the confidentiality of reports relating to the defendant and his organizations contained in various police intelligence files. My only source of unbiased information was from available public documents and from various news media reporters who had, on their own, in the past investigated the defendant and his various organizations.

20. On May 4, 1981, the complaint was amended to add Willis Carto, The Liberty Lobby, and Ditlieb Felderer as defendants.

21. On or about May 8, 1981, I traveled to Washington, DC to retain investigators to examine public documents in that city and to personally serve Willis Carto with a notice to appear at a deposition within the county of his residence, Los Angeles, California.

22. On May 11, 1981, Willis Carto was personally served to appear at my office for deposition on May 21, 1981 and to produce documents. He did not appear, nor was there any communication from counsel on his behalf.

23. On June 3, 1981, the matter was heard in Department 68 of the Superior Court, and upon the defendant's promise to file answers and to produce David McCalden for deposition, the default and motion for sanctions was taken off calendar. On that same day, by amendment, the Independence House, Liberty Lifeline, and the Council on Dangerous Drugs were added as defendants. (MJN #4)

24. On June 12, 1981, the deposition of David McCalden was taken, at which time the personal involvement of Willis Carto in each and every operation of the IHR was fully established. Refer to an analysis of corporate liability filed subsequently in connection with the motion on summary judgment for further details of this involvement. (MJN #5)

25. On or about June 21, 1981, I again traveled to Washington, DC to meet with my investigators. While there, I met for the first time Charles Bermant, an investigative reporter for Jack Anderson. Jack Anderson had for some time been in preparation of a magazine article on Carto, and from Mr. Bermant, I received certain advance information from the article, which was subsequently published.

26. Thereafter, a motion for the Legion for the Survival of Freedom to produce records was made, and on June 26, 1981, the Legion appeared through its attorney and refused to produce documents. (MJN #6)

27. On July 18, 1981, I again met with my investigators in Washington, DC to review their findings from a search of public records.

28. On or about August 17, 1981, Willis Carto became a *de facto* defendant in the Los Angeles lawsuit when he directed interrogatories in his own name to Mr. Mermelstein. Those interrogatories were answered on September 23, 1981. (MJN #7)

29. On August 26, 1981, both plaintiff's and defendants' motions on summary judgment were continued until October 9, 1981 for hearing.

30. On September 8, 1981, I obtained from the Superior Court documents necessary to take the deposition of Willis Carto in Washington, DC, and on September 10, 1981, I met with investigators in that city to arrange service. That service was unsuccessful during the period required by law. (MJN #8)

31. In the defendant's papers opposing plaintiff's motion for summary judgment is the declaration of Willis Carto dated August 22, 1981, in which he reaffirms his belief in the teachings of Francis Parker Yockey as contained in the *Imperium,* implicitly threatened my life with a "loaded pistol," and asserted my membership in a conspiracy of the Anti-Defamation League, the Jewish Defense League, and the Israeli Mossad. (MJN #9)

32. At all times during these proceedings, Willis Carto personally directed the defense of the case, retaining counsel for the served defendants, and providing questions for depositions.

33. On October 9, 1981, motions for summary judgment and plaintiff's motion for judicial notice were heard in Department 88. Following lengthy arguments which were televised by several television networks, Judge Thomas T. Johnson ruled that the Court "takes judicial notice of the fact that Jews were gassed to death at the Auschwitz Concentration Camp in Poland during 1944. This is a fact not reasonably subject to dispute, determinable by resort to sources of reasonable indisputable accuracy." Certain motions by defendants were granted as to certain causes of action with leave to amend regarding *alter ego.* (MJN #10)

34. An amended complaint was filed on November 16, 1981, and demurrers were filed by counsel for the defendants.

35. On November 22, 1981, I received information that Willis Carto was to be personally present in the Los Angeles Area attending an IHR conference. I prepared a service package including the amended

complaint for Willis Carto and the Liberty Lobby. I checked in with the El Segundo Police Department before proceeding to the Hacienda Hotel in the city of El Segundo. Upon my arrival, I located the meeting room of the IHR and was informed that Willis Carto was within. I waited outside until all members left for lunch and then entered. I was informed by Thomas Marcellus that Mr. Carto "had left" and would not accept service.

36. On February 16, 1982, all demurrers filed by defendants were denied in Department 82, and the defendants were directed to answer the amended complaint. (MJN #11)

37. During the months of April, May and June 1982, arrangements were made for the substitution of new counsel for Mr. Mermelstein. Shortly thereafter, I substituted out as counsel of record.

38. In November 1982, I closed my law office.

39. My only contacts during the above period in Washington, DC relating to this case were as the result of Willis Carto's removal of himself from the jurisdiction of the Los Angeles Superior Court, to conduct an investigation of him and his organizations, and to arrange for him to be personally served in discovery proceedings.

40. My contact with Jack Anderson's reporter was as a part of that investigation. The lawsuit filed by Willis Carto against Jack Anderson as the result of that article was dismissed last year.

41. I am further informed and believe that a criminal complaint arising out of a demonstration by the Jewish Defense League at the IHR in 1981 was dismissed when Willis Carto failed to appear to testify in that misdemeanor battery proceeding.

42. A lawsuit brought by Willis Carto and the Liberty Lobby against the Anti-Defamation League was dismissed after extensive discovery by the Liberty Lobby when Willis Carto refused to appear at an ordered deposition. (MJN #12)

43. On or about June 23, 1983, I received by certified mail the first complaint in the present action. At that time, I had been without contact with my former client, Mel Mermelstein, for approximately six months and had not spoken with Herb Brin for almost two years. In the past, I have had only two contacts with any representatives of the Jewish Defense League. Both were with Mr. Irv Ruben. The first was a telephone contact in which I was seeking information during the early stages of the case regarding Willis Carto and his various organizations. I obtained no

information that I was not already aware of. The only other contact I had with Mr. Ruben was on November 22, 1981, when I was attempting to serve Willis Carto at the Hacienda Hotel. The Jewish Defense League began picketing outside the hotel, and I went out and asked Mr. Ruben to leave as he was an embarrassment and was interfering with my attempt of service. He left shortly thereafter and I have had no other contact.

44. On July 12, 1983, I called Mr. Fleming Lee, counsel for the plaintiff. Mr. Lee informed me on that date that an amended complaint had already been filed which would affect the Jewish Defense League only and that I would receive a copy shortly by mail. We agreed that I would have until August 1, 1983 to answer the amended complaint.

45. On or about July 18, 1983, I received the amended complaint by regular mail. This complaint bore a signature purportedly by Fleming Lee which appears to be different than the signature on the original complaint.

46. The amended complaint struck the Jewish Defense League and its two named officers from the title; however, it left all the acts which have been publicly attributed to the Jewish Defense League in the body of the complaint.

47. I was still unable to obtain independent counsel and was contemplating doing the research necessary to appear *in pro per* when I called Mr. Lee again on August 1, 1983 to communicate with him to avoid a default being taken.

48. Mr. Lee advised me that Mr. Carto was very concerned about my answer being received, having just "come downstairs to check on it." He advised me that he would have to check with Mr. Carto but that he would not take a default without first letting me know. He also stated at that time that he had not done an independent investigation of me.

49. On August 11, 1983, I called Mr. Lee. He said that Mr. Carto was very upset and that he could not grant an extension. I told him that I could not possibly respond to the complaint until September 1, 1983; however, that I would do so on about that date.

August 31, 1983

WILLIAM J. COX, *in pro per*

Note from the Author

Although my name may not be particularly well known, many people have heard about my work as a public interest attorney. Particularly because Turner Network Television continues to show a movie about it, the Holocaust Case is fairly well known.

I have always resisted writing about my personal experiences; however, following a serious illness in December 2012, my wife, Helen, increased her encouragement for me to write my memoirs. The following February, we went on our annual retreat, and I vowed I would begin to document the public matters I've been involved in.

I thought about the Holocaust Case and remembered I had filed a lengthy declaration which summarized the background of the defendants and the events which led to the lawsuit. Having published a series of eBooks in 2012, the thought occurred to me that I could easily publish the declaration (Appendix A) for those who might be interested in the history of the case.

As I looked through the files stored in the garage, I discovered I still had the reporter's transcript of the court hearing and the original motion for judicial notice. I also found the subsequent lawsuit in which I was sued by Willis Carto in Washington, DC. The events of that second case have been emotionally suppressed for years; however, with my memory refreshed, I decided the Washington story might also be of some interest and value. All of these documents provided a comprehensive overview of the case, and I set about to write a short backstory about the two cases.

Once I had completed the manuscript and edited the court documents, I asked a friend to review the book for content and grammar. Dr. William (Bill) Younglove is one of those rare, but precious, educators who chose to remain in the classroom educating children, rather than in the office managing teachers. I met him when he worked with Helen at a middle school in a poverty-stricken neighborhood. Since his retirement, Bill has graciously edited my books, including this one. Not only is he an extraordinarily precise, but gentle, editor, he has an extensive background in the history of the Holocaust. He has written numerous articles about Holocaust pedagogy and edited and contributed to several journals on the subject. Bill encouraged me to expand and publish the memoir as a trade paperback.

I am sure David Levinson would take an interest in this book project if he were still with us, and he would certainly have something to say about it. In his place, his wife, journalist Dorothy Korber, graciously reviewed the manuscript in its final stages and made a number of valuable suggestions.

I could not have wrapped up the story without the help and support of these friends, and I could not have completed the original litigation without the dedicated assistance of attorneys Cheryl Bender, Daniel Mangan, Jana Zimmer, Joseph White and Michael Maroko, and journalists David Levinson and Herb Brin.

Finally, nothing I write can be published until it has been thoroughly "Helenized" by my wife, my editor of last resort. I often tell her she would be a much better cross-examiner in court than me, as she asks so many questions in her demand for clarity. I am thankful every day for her presence next to me.

BIBLIOGRAPHY OF SIGNIFICANT WORKS ON THE HOLOCAUST AND ITS DENIAL

Adler, Hans G., *Theresienstadt 1941-1945.* (Wallstein Verlag GmbH, 2005).

Arad, Yitzhak, Ed., Gutman, Yisrael, Ed., & Margaliot, Abraham, Ed., BenDor, Lea, Translator, *Documents on the Holocaust: Selected Sources on the Destruction of the Jews of Germany and Austria, Poland, and the Soviet Union.* (University of Nebraska Press, 1999).

Arendt, Hannah, *Eichmann in Jerusalem: A Report on the Banality of Evil.* (Penguin Classics, 1994).

Atkins, Stephen E., *Holocaust Denial as an International Movement.* (Praeger, 2009).

Bartov, Omer, Ed., *The Holocaust: Origins, Implementation, Aftermath (Rewriting Histories).* (Routledge, 2000).

Berenbaum, Michael J., Ed., & Peck, Abraham, Ed., *The Holocaust and History: The Known, the Unknown, the Disputed, and the Reexamined.* (Indiana University Press, 2002).

Berenbaum, Michael, *The World Must Know: The History of the Holocaust as Told in the United States Holocaust Memorial Museum.* (The Johns Hopkins University Press, 2005).

Black, Edwin, *IBM and the Holocaust: The Strategic Alliance between Nazi German and America's Most Powerful Corporation.* (Crown, 2001).

Bloxham, Donald, *Genocide on Trial - War Crimes Trials and the Formation of Holocaust History and Memory.* (Oxford University Press, 2003).

Broszat, Martin, Krausnick, Helmut, Buchheim, Hans, & Jacobsen, Hans-Adolf, *The Concentration Camps 1933-45.* (Collins, 1968).

Browning, Christopher R., *The Origins of the Final Solution: The Evolution of Nazi Jewish Policy, September 1939 - March 1942 (Comprehensive History of the Holocaust)*. (Bison Books, 2007).

Brudnoy, David, *Viewpoints: The Conservative Alternative*. (Winston Press, 1973), p. 207.

Brustein, William I., *Roots of Hate: Anti-Semitism in Europe Before the Holocaust*. (Cambridge University Press, 2003).

Coogan, Kevin, *Dreamer of the Day: Francis Parker Yockey & The Postwar Fascist International*. (Automedia, 1998).

Dalton, Thomas, *Debating the Holocaust: A New Look at Both Sides*. (Theses & Dissertations Press, 2009).

Dawidowicz, Lucy S., *The Holocaust and the Historians*. (Harvard University Press, 1981).

Dwork, Deborah, & van Pelt, Robert Jan, *Holocaust: A History*. (W. W. Norton & Company, 2003).

Eaglestone, Robert, *Postmodernism and Holocaust Denial (Postmodern Encounters)*. (Icon Books), 1997).

Eaglestone, Robert, *The Holocaust and the Postmodern*. (Oxford University Press, 2008).

Edelheit, Abraham J., Edelheit, Hershel, & Edelheit, Ann, *History of the Holocaust: A Handbook and Dictionary*. (Westview Press, 1995).

Epstein, Eric Joseph & Rosen, Philip, *Dictionary of the Holocaust: Biography, Geography, and Terminology*. (Greenwood Press, 1997).

Evans, Richard J., *Lying About Hitler*. (Basic Books, 2002).

Evans, Richard J., *Telling Lies About Hitler: The Holocaust, History and the David Irving Trial*. (Verso Books, 2002).

Favez, Jean-Claude, (Translated by John and Beryl Fletcher), *The Red Cross and the Holocaust*. (Cambridge University Press, 1999).

Friedlander, Saul, *Nazi Germany and the Jews, 1939-1945: The Years of Extermination*. (Harper Perennial, 2008).

Gerstenfeld, Manfred, *The Multiple Distortions of Holocaust Memory*. (Jewish Political Review, 19:3-4, October 28, 2007).

Gilbert, Sir Martin, *The Holocaust: A History of the Jews of Europe During the Second World War*. (Holt Paperbacks, 1987).

Gutman, Ysrael, *Anatomy of the Auschwitz Death Camp*, (Indiana University Press, 1998).

Guttenplan, D. D., *The Holocaust on Trial*. (W. W. Norton & Company, 2001).

Hilberg, Raul, *The Destruction of the European Jews*. (Holmes & Meier, 1985).

Hochstadt, Steve, *Sources of the Holocaust (Documents in History)*. (Palgrave Macmillan, 2004).

Hoess, Rudolf, Levi, Primo (Introduction), *Commandant of Auschwitz*. (Phoenix, 2000)

Iofis, Moshe, *Germany's Leaders Against Holocaust Denial and Anti-Semitism: A Salient Day in the German Bundestag*. (Xlibris, 2011).

Kahn, Robert, *Holocaust Denial and the Law: A Comparative Study*. (Palgrave Macmillan, 2004).

Kaplan, Marion A., *Between Dignity and Despair: Jewish Life in Nazi Germany*. (Oxford University Press, 1999).

Kaye, Ephraim, *Desecraters of Memory (Confronting Holocaust Denial)*. (Yad Vashem; 1st edition, 1997).

Kokh, Alfred, Ed., *Denial of the Denial, or the Battle of Auschwitz: Debates About the Demography and Geo-Politics of the Holocaust*. (Academic Studies Press, 2011).

Kren, George M., & Rapoport, Leon, *The Holocaust and the Crisis of Human Behavior*. (Holmes and Meier, 1980).

Kuttner, Paul, *The Holocaust: Hoax or History?: The Book of Answers to Those Who Would Deny the Holocaust*. (Dawnwood Press, 1997).

Landau, Ronnie S., *The Nazi Holocaust: Its History and Meaning*. (I. B. Tauris, 2006).

Laqueur, Walter, Ed. & Baumel, Judith Tydor, Ed. *The Holocaust Encyclopedia*. (Yale University Press, 2001).

Lipstadt, Deborah E., *Denying the Holocaust: The Growing Assault on Truth and Memory*. (Plume, 1994).

Littman, Solomon, *Holocaust Denial: Bigotry in the Guise of Scholarship*. (Simon Wiesenthal Center, 1994).

Litvak, Meir, *From Empathy to Denial: Arab Responses to the Holocaust (Columbia/Hurst)*. (Columbia University Press, 2009).

London, Louise, *Whitehall and the Jews: 1933-1948: British Immigration Policy, Jewish Refugees and the Holocaust*. (Cambridge University Press, 2003).

Mankowitz, Zeev W., *Life Between Memory and Hope: the Survivors of the Holocaust and Occupied Germany*. (Cambridge University Press, 2002).

Mermelstein, Mel, *By Bread Alone: The Story of A-4685, Mel Mermelstein, A Survivor of the Nazi Holocaust*. (Auschwitz Study Foundation, 1993).

Michael, George, *Willis Carto and the American Far Right*. (University Press of Florida, 2008).

Moyn, Samuel, *A Holocaust Controversy: The Treblinka Affair in Postwar France (Tauber Institue Series for the Study of European Jewry)*. (Brandeis, 2005).

Neville, Peter, *The Holocaust (Cambridge Perspectives in History)*. (Cambridge University Press, 1999).

Niewyk, Donald, *The Holocaust: Problems and Perspectives of Interpretation (Problems in European Civilization (Wadsworth))*. (Cengage Learning, 2010).

Novick, Peter, *The Holocaust in American Life*. (Mariner Books, 2000).

Reitlinger, Gerald, *The Final Solution: The Attempt to Exterminate the Jews of Europe, 1939-1945*. (University of Michigan Library, 2009).

Rhodes, Richard, *Masters of Death: The SS-Einsatzgruppen and the Invention of the Holocaust*. (Vintage, 2003).

Rosenbaum, Alan S., *Is the Holocaust Unique?: Perspectives on Comparative Genocide*. (Westview Press, 1997).

Rosenfeld, Alvin H., *The End of the Holocaust*. (Indiana University Press, 2011).

Kaufman, Debra, G. Herman, D. Phillips and J. Ross (eds.) *From the Protocols of the Elders of Zion to Holocaust Denial Trials: Challenging the Media, the Law and the Academy*. (Valentine Mitchell, 2007).

Rothberg, Michael, *Multidirectional Memory: Remembering the Holocaust in the Age of Decolonization (Cultural Memory in the Present)*. (Stanford University Press, 2009).

Rubenstein, Richard L., & Roth, John K., *Approaches to Auschwitz: The Holocaust and Its Legacy*. (Westminister John Knox Press, 2003).

Rupprecht, Nancy, Ed., & Koenig, Wendy, Ed., *Holocaust Persecution: Responses and Consequences*. (Cambridge Scholars Publishing, 2010).

Sciolino, Anthony J., *The Holocaust, the Church, and the Law of Unintended Consequences: How Christian Anti-Judaism Spawned Nazi Anti-Semitism.* (iUniverse, 2012).

Seidel, Gill, *Holocaust Denial: Anti-Semitism, Racism and the New Right.* (Beyond the Pale Publications, 1986).

Shapiro, Shelly, Ed., *Truth Prevails: Demolishing Holocaust Denial: The End of the Leuchter Report.* (Beate Klarsfeld Foundation, 1990).

Shermer, Michael, & Grobman, Alex, Hertzberg, Arthur (Foreward), *Denying History: Who Says the Holocaust Never Happened and Why Do They Say It?* (University of California Press, 2009).

Stern, Kenneth S., *Holocaust Denial.* (American Jewish Committee, 1993).

Sussman, Robert Wald, *The Myth of Race: The Troubling Persistence of an Unscientific Idea.* (Harvard University Press, 2014).

Swartz, Terese Pencak, *Holocaust Forgotten - Five Million Non-Jewish Victims (Volume 1).* (CreateSpace Independent Publishing Platform, 2012).

van Pelt, Robert Jan, *The Case for Auschwitz: Evidence from the Irving Trial,* (Indiana University Press, 2002)

Vidal-Naquet, Pierre, *Assassins of Memory: Essays on the Denial of the Holocaust (European Perspectives: A Series in Social Thought and Cultural Criticism).* (Columbia University Press, 1993).

Weissmark, Mona Sue, *Justice Matters: Legacies of the Holocaust and World War II.* (Oxford University Press, 2004).

Weinding, Paul Julian, *Epidemics and Genocide in Eastern Europe 1890-1945.* (Oxford University Press, 2000).

Wistrich, Robert S., *Holocaust Denial: The Politics of Perfidy.* (de Gruyter, 2012).

Zeskind, Leonard, *Blood and Politics: The History of the White Nationalist Movement from the Margins to the Mainstream.* (Farrar, Straus and Giroux, 2009).

Zimmerman, John C., *Holocaust Denial: Demographics, Testimonies and Ideologies.* (University Press of America, 2000).

ABOUT THE AUTHOR

For more than 50 years, William John Cox has written extensively on law, politics, philosophy and the human condition. During that time, he vigorously pursued a career in law enforcement, public policy, and the law.

As a police officer, Cox was an early leader in the "New Breed" movement to professionalize law enforcement. He wrote the *Policy Manual* of the Los Angeles Police Department and the role of the police in America for the Nixon administration.

As an attorney, Cox worked for the U.S. Department of Justice to implement national criminal justice standards and goals, prosecuted cases for the Los Angeles County District Attorney's Office, and operated a public interest law practice.

In 1979, Cox filed a class-action lawsuit on behalf of all citizens directly in the U.S. Supreme Court alleging the government no longer represented the People who elected it. In 1981, representing a Jewish survivor of Auschwitz, Cox investigated and successfully sued a group of radical right-wing organizations which denied the Holocaust. He published the suppressed Dead Sea Scrolls in 1991 on behalf of a "secret" client.

Cox retired in 2007 as a Supervising Trial Counsel for the State Bar of California, where he led a team of attorneys and investigators which prosecuted attorneys accused of serious misconduct and criminal gangs engaged in the illegal practice of law.

He can be contacted through his website, www.williamjohncox.com.

Made in the USA
Middletown, DE
27 November 2015